Active LE
Curriculum for Excellence

Third Level
HISTORY
Course Notes

Neil McLennan

CONTENTS

CONTENTS

INTRODUCTION

Whilst this book is divided into outcomes and experiences as outlines in *Curriculum for Excellence*, it would perhaps be unwise not to take a topic based approach. The themes of the outcomes permeate the topics in each chapter. However, teachers teach best and learners learn best when skills and themes are pinned to what is the joy of History and history teaching... the story.

Scotland's story is a unique and fascinating one. Whilst the curriculum should not, and is not, Scotland focussed it is vital that we should provide students with a clear understanding of where we have come from. It is only with this understanding that the young people can take this country forward. The book is not merely coverage of Scottish History. Numerous attempts have been made to link Scotland with the wider world.

Some chapters cover familiar themes and I make no apology for this. I would be unable to write a textbook for the History curriculum in Scotland without covering some familiar ground. For example the geography of our nation defines us. Being part of an island would necessitate study of the Vikings invaders and later our domination of the sea via the shipbuilding industry. Our relations with our English neighbours define us in many cultural ways and so coverage of conflict and cooperation within and outwith the Union also feature. The Scottish Wars of Independence unit may be seen by some as 'History by *Braveheart*'. However, we need to cover such as a turning point politically, militarily and culturally. The people and events of this era contributed much to the development of the Scottish nation we live in today. Further, History should be taught with a BANG and with some sort of WOW factor for the young people sat in our classrooms. What better unit to study than the Wars of Independence?

However in including some topics I have of course had to omit some others. There is little mention of the lowlands in the Examining Evidence section. The Highland Clearances were chosen due to their ability to engage students in active debate and one which is ongoing even to this day. Likewise I have not given anywhere near enough attention to the issues surrounding Empire, Emigration and Immigration. This was design as these are still in the 'court phase' of history with researchers still breaking new ground. As such, this book has very much so covered the domestic history of Scotland. Once the dust has settled on the wider 'Scotland and the World' debate then perhaps a second edition can be produced, or better still a new textbook produced which focuses on wider European and World History, but with distinctive Scottish twist. National Qualification students do now study some of these topics in isolation as part of optional National Qualification studies. However, it would be nice to ensure students were exposed to these areas as part of their compulsory education.

I hope learners and teachers will not only find these tasks interesting but also fun and enjoyable. My experience of trying some of them out has brought fun, laugher and at different times tears of emotion and of joy.

I hope you also will enjoy them either as a student, a member of staff or perhaps an interested reader.

Neil Douglas Roderick McLennan, Edinburgh, May 2010

HOW TO USE THIS BOOK

Leckie & Leckie's Active Learning series has been developed specifically to provide teachers, students and parents with the ability to implement the Curriculum for Excellence as effectively as possible. Each book has been written with the following objectives in mind:

- To support the implementation of Curriculum for Excellence in schools.
- To engage students by taking a contextualised learning approach and providing a range of rich task activities.
- To assist teachers with the planning and delivery of lessons and assessment.

For the Third Level History Outcomes and Experiences, both a Course Notes book and an accompanying Activity Book have been published.

COVERING CURRICULUM FOR EXCELLENCE

Active History Course Notes comprehensively covers the Third Level Outcomes and Experiences for History, within the Social Sciences.

The Outcomes and Experiences have been organised into chapters, with a different topic covered on each double page spread. The Outcome and Experience reference number for each topic appears in the table of contents.

Every double page spread opens with a knowledge summary for a particular topic which conveys key ideas and concepts. The key topic knowledge is enhanced by practical examples, illustration or case study to reinforce learning. *Top Tips* and facts are also included to highlight key information. Think time offers students a chance for reflection.

ADDRESSING THE PRIORITIES OF CURRICULUM FOR EXCELLENCE

Active History Course Notes focuses on methods to implement the philosophy underpinning Curriculum for Excellence. It addresses the Curriculum for Excellence in a thoroughly practical way that makes learning both engaging and fun!

- Ideas for rich task activities are provided for every topic to enable pupils to gain skills and experiences as well as to achieve learning outcomes.
- Paired and group learning activities encourage students to take responsibility for and direct their own learning, whilst developing the four capacities.
- Creative ideas are offered for making cross-disciplinary links with other classroom subjects, both within the Social Sciences and more widely, to help ensure students join up their learning.

- The relevance of each topic to everyday life is highlighted in order to help students transfer their skills and knowledge to other areas of their lives.
- Extension activities are included in the Did You Know? boxes to encourage students' interest and develop breadth and depth of learning.

The toolkit of ideas, subject links and activities contained in *Active History Course Notes* can be used in the classroom and/or at home.

Each double page spread includes the following features:

Activities column: this column contains questions to assess knowledge and understanding as well as rich tasks to deepen understanding of each topic.

Make the Link box: this box highlights the relevance of the topic to a number of other school subjects. This enables learners to gain a more holistic understanding of each topic.

Our Everyday Lives box: this box provides an example of how each topic relates to real life, in order to demonstrate its practical relevance.

Did You Know? box: this box contains an additional fact about each topic to engage further interest and to bring the subject to life. It can also be used as an extension activity to broaden and deepen learning.

ASSESSMENT

The accompanying *Active History Activity Book* contains an assessment checklist for each topic based around the Third Level Outcomes and Experiences. It also provides:

- Self-assessment mind maps to encourage students to reflect on their learning and their development of the four capacities.
- Ideas for inter-disciplinary projects, which include success criteria and estimated timelines.
- Rich task activities around each topic to bring learning to life.
- Differentiated revision questions to check knowledge and understanding for each topic.

SUPPORTING TEACHERS AND STUDENTS

The *Active History Course Notes* book sets out to provide teachers and students with a valuable toolkit of easy-to-implement ideas for incorporating the philosophies of Curriculum for Excellence into teaching and learning.

The highlighted links with other subjects, activities ideas and real life examples are the perfect starting point for teachers and students to build upon and develop as they explore a topic. At Leckie & Leckie, our intention is that this *Course Notes* book will inspire learners to investigate subjects widely and deeply in practical and creative ways.

KEY FEATURES

Each double page spread contains the following key features:

MAKE THE LINK
draws out links between subjects on a particular topic to aid interdisciplinary learning and deepen understanding

DID YOU KNOW?
boxes provide interesting and engaging facts about each topic to help build knowledge

OUR EVERYDAY LIVES
Illustrates how the knowledge translates into practical examples drawn from real life

ACTIVITES TO TRY
Short and engaging revision questions and rich tasks

EXAMPLE
Examples given are captivating and spark students' interest

TOP TIP
Key facts and concepts are highlighted to aid knowledge retention

KEY WORDS
Most important words and phrases highlighted in bold

FULL-COLOUR
Bright and stimulating colour throughout

TIMELINES

Timelines are used all the time by lots of different people. When you are at secondary school you have a timeline showing each class you go to each day. It is called your timetable. You could even make up a timeline which shows everything you did from the moment you got out of bed in the morning until the time you went back to bed at night.

Timelines are very useful for showing things that have happened and the time at which they happened.

Historians use timelines to show events over a long period of time – much longer than your school timetable, which only shows a day or week of classes. A historian's timeline might show things happening over hundreds or even thousands of years!

BC after a year means the number of years **b**efore **C**hrist was born. AD before a year comes from the Latin, **A**nno **D**omini. This means the number of years after the birth of Christ.

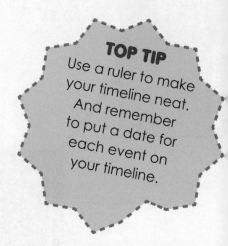

TOP TIP
Use a ruler to make your timeline neat. And remember to put a date for each event on your timeline.

8

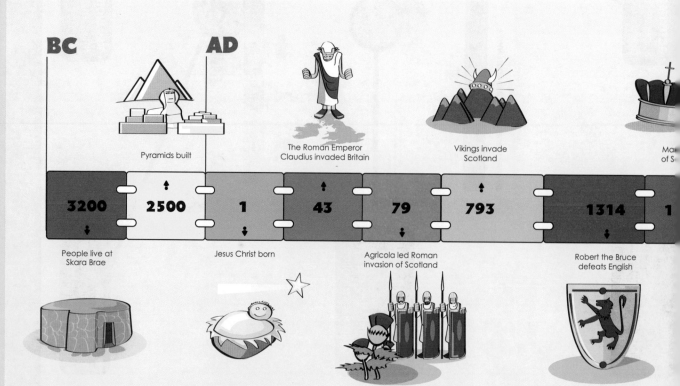

BC   **AD**

Pyramids built

The Roman Emperor Claudius invaded Britain

Vikings invade Scotland

Ma of S

| 3200 | 2500 | 1 | 43 | 79 | 793 | 1314 | 1 |

People live at Skara Brae

Jesus Christ born

Agricola led Roman invasion of Scotland

Robert the Bruce defeats English

WHY PEOPLE SETTLED *

ACTIVITIES

1 a) What two things do timelines show?
   b) What do AD and BC stand for?
   c) Which event is the most recent on the timeline?
   d) Which event took place longest ago on the timeline?
   e) How many years are there between Mary Queen of Scots being born and the Scottish Parliament reopening?
   f) How many years are there between the first Vikings in Scotland and the first people living at Skara Brae?
   g) How many years are there between the Roman and the Viking invasions of Scotland?

2 What famous event would you add to the timeline? What year did it take place?
   With your class, make a timeline showing the events you have all chosen.

   Or…

   Select a famous person in history and make a timeline showing the key events in their life.

Scotland and England
have same parliament

603 | 1707 | 1999 | Today

d and England
e same king

Scottish Parliament
reopens

WHY HAVE PEOPLE SETTLED IN SCOTLAND?

MAKE THE LINK

Everyone in a school uses timelines each day – teachers and pupils all have timetables so they know what they are doing at different times in the day!

In **Home Economics**, timelines are used when you are following a recipe to know when to start cooking and preparing different foods.

In **Science** we use timelines to show the evolution of man. Also, scientists use timelines to help them when they are doing experiments. When they are doing a new experiment they will make up a new timeline that shows what happens at each stage.

In **Craft and Design** you use timelines when you are making something like a chair. It shows what you should be doing and when you should be doing it.

9

DID YOU KNOW?

Pre history is the word we use when looking at events that happened before mankind wrote anything down. We can find out what happened at this time by looking at pictures and symbols people left behind.

OUR EVERYDAY LIVES:

Air-traffic controllers have to use timelines to know when planes should be coming in to land and taking off. They have to be very skilful as sometimes planes are late or early when this happens the timelines have to be changed. They must think quickly and change things on their timeline so everything runs smoothly in our airports.

WHAT HAPPENED AT SKARA BRAE?

3200 BC Settlers at Skara Brae	2500 BC Pyramids built	43 AD Romans invade Britain	795 AD Viking attacks	today

In 1850 a winter storm blew over the Orkney Islands just north of the mainland of Scotland. On the beach at Orkney the high winds caused a huge sandstorm. After the storm, sand on the beach had been blown away to reveal an ancient stone village called Skara Brae.

The village is believed to be around 4000 years old! In the village there are eight stone houses. Why would anyone want to live in Skara Brae, or even Scotland, when it is a cold, windy and wet place? It is our job as historians to find out.

Look at the map. Why do you think people would want to stay at Skara Brae? After all it is so far away!

Between 8000 BC and 4000 BC is called the Mesolithic Age. People in Scotland were hunter gatherers, people moved around the country with no real home. They were nomads who simply wandered in search of food. The Neolithic Age (4000 BC to 2000 BC) was when people settled in one place and set up farms. The people of Skara Brae were probably early day farmers. They survived on the food they produced. The area they chose to live in was perfect. It was near the sea for fishing, transport and trade (buying and selling things). Also, it had lots of good farmland. The early farmers started to use stone tools. Later on we will find Scots using bronze and then iron to help them. Iron, of course, continues to be used today.

Historians are people who find out about what happened in the past. Archaeologists are people who search for objects from the past to help us find out about how people lived many years ago. They are like historians but they go digging for clues. Archaeologists search for objects which they call artefacts. Imagine you were one of the first archaeologists sent to the village to find out about the people who lived there thousands of years ago. What sorts of questions would you want to ask about Skara Brae?

Archaeologists use lots of tools to help them. They have to be very careful when digging. As they get closer to the artefact they are more careful because it is so fragile.

10

WHY PEOPLE SETTLED *

ACTIVITIES

1 Complete the following table

Skara Brae Facts	
Who lived here?	
When did they live here?	
Why did they live here?	
How did they survive?	
What did they work as?	

2 If you met a villager who had lived at Skara Brae thousands of years ago what other questions would you ask him/her? Make up a list of five questions.

3 Below is a list of tools archaeologists use in their search for items from the past. Decide in what order the archaeologists would use them. The first one is done for you.

Tool	When used
Wheelbarrow	
Trowel	
Toothbrush	
Large brush	
Spade	First

REMEMBER: as they get closer of the artefact they must be more careful, so not to damage anything.

MAKE THE LINK

In **Science** we look at the sort of food people need to survive. What sort of food did people at Skara Brae eat? Did they have similar food chains to the ones we have today? Also, **Biology** lessons may look at the work of forensic detectives and how science is used to find out about the past.

In **Art** we learn about design and colour. Try to find some pictures of the objects discovered at Skara Brae. Look at their design. What sorts of colours do you think were used in their art work? How did they make these artefacts given that they only had stone tools? How have designs changed over time?

In **Maths** we learn about grids and coordinates. Archaeologists use these as well when they first discover a new site they want to investigate. They must set up a grid over the site so that they can record and log what is found and where.

DID YOU KNOW?

Did you know the village at Skara Brae was built long before the Egyptians had started to build the Pyramids? Historians think people lived at Skara Brae from around 3200 BC to 2500 BC whereas the first Pyramid was built some time around 2500 BC.

OUR EVERYDAY LIVES:

The police often use archaeologists and forensic scientists to help investigate crimes. Detectives ask the same sorts of questions as historians and archaeologists would ask about Skara Brae. We call these questions the **5W** questions you can see these in activity 1 on this page (who, when, where, why, what).

PRIMARY AND SECONDARY SOURCES

In the last lesson we found that historians are people who find out about what happened in the past. We said that they are a bit like police detectives. Detectives look for clues after a crime. Historians also look for clues but they call their clues **sources**. Historians use two types of sources, and they are both very important when trying to find out about the past.

The first type of source is a **primary source**. Primary sources are clues that have come from the time the historian is investigating. For example, if historians were trying to find out what it was like to live in Britain during the Second World War they might look at a gas mask. The gas mask comes from the Second World War so it is a primary source. Another example of a primary source from the Second World War is the diary of Anne Frank. Because Anne Frank wrote the diary during the Second World War it is a primary source. Primary sources are useful for us finding out about the past. They can also be very valuable because they are so old.

A **secondary source** is completely different. A secondary source is something that was made long after the event the historian is investigating. For example, if you wrote a story about what happened to the people of Skara Brae this would be a secondary source. It is a secondary source because it was made long after the people lived there and you were not there at the time. So secondary sources are made after the time you are investigating.

Sources to help us investigate the Skara Brae mystery:

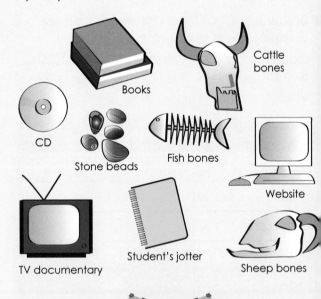

Books

Cattle bones

CD

Stone beads

Fish bones

Website

TV documentary

Student's jotter

Sheep bones

TOP TIP

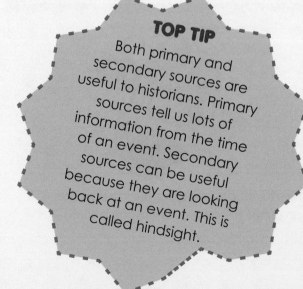

Both primary and secondary sources are useful to historians. Primary sources tell us lots of information from the time of an event. Secondary sources can be useful because they are looking back at an event. This is called hindsight.

12

WHY PEOPLE SETTLED *

ACTIVITIES

1 Complete the following table using the items from the opposite page. Decide if each one is a primary or secondary source. The first has been done for you.

Item	Primary source	Secondary source
Fish bones	✓	
TV documentary		
CD rom		
Book		
Stone beads		
Sheep bones		
Cattle bones		

2 Copy the following sentence and then complete one sentence for each source above:

The CD Rom is a primary secondary source because *it was made after the time people lived at Skara Brae.*

3 Look at the list of sources you have put into the table. Decide which one is the most useful to historians. Which item tells us the most about Skara Brae? Be able to explain your choice.

4 With a partner, discuss the other sources in your table. What do the other items tell us about Skara Brae? Are they useful in any way when helping us to find out about the past?

WHY HAVE PEOPLE SETTLED IN SCOTLAND?

MAKE THE LINK

In **Computing Studies** we find out how to use the internet and websites. There are lots of sites out there from which we can find out useful information but we need to be very careful when using the web. How you can be sure that the website you are using is useful and contains correct information.

In **Science** we find out how scientists use carbon dating to tell how old an item actually is. This is a technique that archaeologists use on sources which they cannot date exactly.

In **Art and Design** we look at lots of different images and pictures. Some are about events that happened in the past. How can we tell if the pictures were drawn at the time or if they were drawn long after the event they are portraying?

13

DID YOU KNOW?

Photographs can be useful sources for historians. The first black and white photographs were taken in 1826 by Frenchman Joseph Nicéphore Niépce. In 1908 Gabriel Lippmann from Luxembourg won the Nobel Prize in Physics for developing colour photographs. All the photographs we have of Skara Brae are from recent times and only show what is left of the houses. The people who lived there would not have had cameras!

OUR EVERYDAY LIVES:

Antique shops sell items from the past which can be very valuable. People will sometimes pay thousands, if not millions, of pounds for original items that come from the past. However, there are many fakes out there which are made to look like they come from long ago.

SKARA BRAE HOUSES

The village at Skara Brae was left exactly as it was thousands of years ago. It is as though the people had left only yesterday. In total, eight houses were found at Skara Brae. The houses are very similar to our own houses in some ways and in other ways they are very different.

The houses were built in two lines and seemed to be facing each other. Some people think they did this to stop the wind getting into the houses. The Orkney Islands are a very windy place as we already know from the storm in 1850. It is so stormy and windy in Orkney that few trees can survive there.

The houses were not built from wood but from stone. The roofs were made of whalebones covered in turf. Archaeologists found two holes at either side of the door and think a long wooden or bone object was used to lock the door.

Look at the picture below and look at the labels around the picture. Think about which areas of the house were used for what things. Decide which areas of the house are similar as our houses today and which areas are different.

TOP TIP

Most of history is about comparing how things have changed with what has stayed the same. When things stay the same this is called **continuity**. **Change** is when things become different. Both words and ideas are very important for us to know.

14

Bed

Fish store

Fire place

Dressing table

WHY PEOPLE SETTLED *

ACTIVITIES

1 From your own knowledge make a list of reasons why people move house today.

2 Use your knowledge from previous lesson to make a list of reasons why people may have moved to Skara Brae.

3 Make a list of all the materials used to make a Skara Brae house.

4 Complete the following table showing the differences between your house and the houses at Skara Brae. Use the information on the page opposite and the photograph to help you.

Features of house	Skara Brae house	My house
Number of rooms		
Protection from the weather		
Security		
Living area		
Where to cook		
Where to sleep		
Where to store food		
Where to store personal items		
Walls		
Roof		

WHY HAVE PEOPLE SETTLED IN SCOTLAND?

MAKE THE LINK

Home Economics, Art and **Craft and Design** all may look at tools used for everyday cooking and housework. Designers of everyday tools need to think about making them easy to use and practical. They also have to design them to catch people's eyes and make people want to buy them.

In **Craft, Design and Technology** you may make some items which can be used in your house. The materials you use may be very similar to those used at Skara Brae. However, the tools you use will be very different. Remember, Skara Brae villagers would be using stone. Bronze and iron tools were not used in Scotland until later on.

DID YOU KNOW?

All of the houses at Skara Brae are the same except one. Known as house eight, this house is slightly larger and appears to have been decorated on the walls. There are no beds or storage units in this house. What do you think this house was used for?

OUR EVERYDAY LIVES:

Interior designers work to design the layout of rooms, decoration and where furniture should be placed in each room. Today more and more people are using designs and ideas from the past to give their homes a historic feel.

Old houses can sometimes be very expensive.

WHY DID THE PEOPLE LEAVE SKARA BRAE?

There is lots of evidence about Skara Brae village. The question that remains to be answered is, why did all the people leave? All of the evidence remains like pieces from a jigsaw puzzle.

The evidence needs to be examined to help us come up with some ideas about why people left Skara Brae village. It is your job to come up with some answers. Look at the evidence below and use it to help you to complete the table.

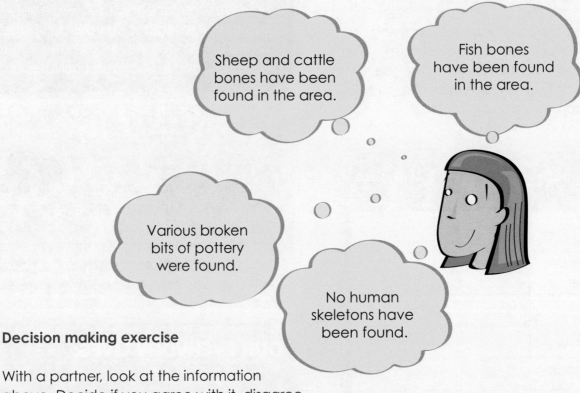

Sheep and cattle bones have been found in the area.

Fish bones have been found in the area.

Various broken bits of pottery were found.

No human skeletons have been found.

Decision making exercise

With a partner, look at the information above. Decide if you agree with it, disagree with it or are unsure. Then copy and complete the table below.

	Agree	Disagree	Unsure
The people of Skara Brae went fishing.			
The people of Skara Brae were highly skilled.			
The people of Skara Brae were killed in a flood.			
The people of Skara Brae were killed in a fire.			
The people of Skara Brae were killed in a war.			
The people of Skara Brae thought they would be coming back to their houses.			

16

WHY PEOPLE SETTLED *

ACTIVITIES

1 For each piece of information in the table, be able to tell the class which box you ticked and give a reason for your decision. For example: *The people of Skara Brae went fishing. I know this because fish bones were found.*

2 Is there any piece of evidence you would like to know more about? What sort of questions would you ask?

3 With a partner, make up a story called 'What happened to the people of Skara Brae?' Use the evidence to help you answer this question.

WHY HAVE PEOPLE SETTLED IN SCOTLAND?

MAKE THE LINK

In **Business Studies** and **Modern Studies** we look at how our choices and decisions are influenced by the ways which we are informed.

In **English** we look at how our opinion is influenced before we developed our informed view.

DID YOU KNOW?

Since the settlers at Skara Brae developed fishing ideas, Scotland has become a major country for fishing and fish farming. Scottish fishermen catch well over half the fish caught in British waters.

17

OUR EVERYDAY LIVES:

It is quite clear why people settled at Skara Brae. However finding out why they left is more difficult. Where do you think they went to? Everyday people move home or even country for a variety of reasons.

FACTS AND OPINIONS ABOUT THE VIKINGS

A fact is something that cannot be changed. For example, 'the grass is green'. If you asked a hundred people they would all have to agree with you because this is true. Therefore, this is a fact. An opinion is something that someone thinks or feels. For example, 'football is great' or 'City High School has the best hockey team'. Not everyone would agree with these statements. They are just what some people think or feel. Statements that have feeling words in them are opinions.

Long after the people of Skara Brae left their village the Vikings arrived in Scotland. The Vikings did lots of things in Scotland. Some of the things they did we all agree on, so these are called facts.

For example, the date they arrived (AD 795) is a fact. That they came to Scotland from Norway and Denmark is a fact. However, there are also lots of opinions about them. Some people think they were bloodthirsty warriors who were scary and caused lots of damage. Not everyone agrees with that statement so it is an opinion. It is based on people's feelings rather than information that everyone agrees on.

People who say that all Vikings were bloodthirsty fighters are **stereotyping** them. This means they are putting them all into one category. It is like saying 'all boys are badly behaved' or 'all girls like pink'. Another stereotype would be that all Scots wear kilts and have ginger hair. Clearly not all Scots are like this so it is a stereotype.

Look at the statements below and decide which ones are facts and which ones are opinions. Try to be careful when you are doing this – do not stereotype Vikings.

Remains of Vikings in Scotland were found buried with axes, arrows, swords and shields.

Some Vikings settled in Scotland as farmers.

The Vikings travelled in long ships.

The Vikings were savages who brutally killed Scots.

The Vikings were nice people who left nice things behind.

The Vikings horrifically burned down our churches.

Vikings came to Scotland because living conditions were good.

The Vikings drank lots of beer.

Many place names in Shetland were changed from Celtic names to Viking ones.

The Vikings attacked Scotland in the late eighth and ninth centuries.

Vikings mercilessly took Scots people as slaves.

Vikings loved poetry, art and also wrote out rules and laws.

18

WHY PEOPLE SETTLED *

ACTIVITIES

1 Identify which statements on the previous page are facts and which statements are opinions. You should set your answer out like this:

Facts about Vikings	Opinions about Vikings

2 In your own words describe the difference between a fact and an opinion.

3 List two possible reasons why the Vikings came to Scotland.

TOP TIP

The people coming into a country are called immigrants. The people leaving a country are called emigrants. An easy way to learn this is to remember that the people coming **i**n start with an '**i**' and those **e**xiting start with an '**e**'.

WHY HAVE PEOPLE SETTLED IN SCOTLAND?

MAKE THE LINK

In **English** it is important that you can detect the differences between fact and opinion when you are reading books, magazines and articles.

In **Modern Studies** you might look at examples of occasions when newspapers, politicians or adverts are biased in order to get their point of view across.

In **Business Education** you could look at how companies are biased in their advertising to get potential customers to buy their products.

DID YOU KNOW?

Up Hellya takes place in Shetland once a year on the last Tuesday in January. It is a festival to celebrate the links between the Shetland Islands and the Scandinavian countries that the Vikings came from. Links between the Shetlands and Scandinavia go back to *when Scandinavian countries owned the Shetland Islands.* At the end of the festival a Viking longship is set on fire.

OUR EVERYDAY LIVES:

Every day, new people move to Scotland from many different countries across the world. Like the Vikings, they have many reasons for coming to Scotland. Some leave their own country because they are pushed out. Some are attracted to Scotland. They are pulled towards our country.

DETECTING BIAS

You found out in the last section how it is important for historians to be able to identify facts and opinions. Opinions can be useful for historians when they are trying to find out about the past, but they can also be very misleading. When someone tries to share with someone else an unfair opinion it can cause confusion.

For example, on Monday mornings websites, forums and newspapers contain references to what happened at weekend football matches. They all tell different stories about what happened.

For example, one newspaper report from a man's premier league match might read:

However, a forum might read:

ROVERS
The best football team

| Home | Forum | Football | Contact |

Welcome

The note

Rovers were cheated once again today when they visited old rivals United. United striker Kennedy was lucky to score a goal. The referee was a joke and he cheated all through the game. Did anyone else see the game and think he cheated as well? It was never a penalty.

International News

The WORLD

United Win

United beat Rovers 1-0 with a superb goal from United striker Craig Kennedy. Kennedy scored a penalty in the 57th minute. The match was watched by 17,000 spectators and puts United top of the league again.

United beat Rovers 1-0 with a superb goal from United striker Craig Kennedy. Kennedy scored a penalty in the 57th minute. The match was watched by 17,000 spectators and puts United top of the league again. United beat Rovers 1-0 with a superb goal from United striker Craig Kennedy. Kennedy scored a penalty in the 57th minute. The match was watched by 17,000 spectators and puts United top of the league again.

We can clearly see that the newspaper report contains mainly facts about the game. On the other hand, the forum contains a lot of opinions and these are biased because they are unfair or one-sided opinions of the game.

WHY PEOPLE SETTLED *

ACTIVITIES

1. a) Explain what a fact is.
   b) Explain what an opinion is.
   c) Explain what bias means.

2. Read the newspaper report and make a list of facts contained in the report.

   Read the website forum page and make a list of opinions contained in the forum.

3. Using the two reports, make up your own factual report of the match.

WHY HAVE PEOPLE SETTLED IN SCOTLAND?

MAKE THE LINK

In **English** you might look at biased reporting of events and persuasive writing. Find stories written by people who have moved from one country to another. Find stories written by people who live in a country they have moved to. Often we can find biased or unfair opinions in these types of stories. In **Religious and Moral Education** you might look at how groups are persecuted by biased reports written about them and unfair words used to describe them.

In **Music** you may look at how music can be used to persuade you or change your mind on something. Are the words of the song also biased when this happens? You might look at the sort of music immigrants to a new country listen to. Do they listen to music sometimes to remind themselves of the country they have come from? People who have emigrated from Scotland might listen to bagpipes in their new country.

21

DID YOU KNOW?

People come and go from Scotland all the time. Many Scots have moved overseas. Robert Gordon was one such man. He made his money as a trader in Gdansk, Poland. On his return he set up a university that is still famous today.

OUR EVERYDAY LIVES:

Scotland is today a multicultural society with many races, religions and nationalities. This began when Celts first came to our country from Europe, Romans from Europe and Vikings from Scandinavia. All immigrant groups have contributed something different to Scotland.

WHAT WAS THE ROMAN EMPIRE?

3200 BC	78 AD	80 AD	122 AD	142 AD	today
Settlers at Skara Brae	Agricol becomes emperor	Romans attack Britain	Hadrians Wall built	Antonine Wall built	

An **empire** is created when one country takes over and controls other countries' lands. The land that is taken over becomes part of the empire. The areas of land taken over are called **colonies**.

In the ancient world there were many great civilisations or groups of people. The Romans, Greeks and Egyptians were some of these great civilisations. The Romans built up a massive empire. At the centre of the empire was Rome. Rome is the capital city of modern day Italy. The Roman Empire stretched as far as Europe, Asia and North Africa. According to **legend**, Rome was founded by Romulus. Romulus and his twin brother, Remus, were taken from their mother and left to starve. A wolf found the two babies and looked after them like a mother until they were old enough to look after themselves. Then Mars, the God of War, told the boys to build a city. The boys had a disagreement and fought with each other. The winner was Romulus, so the city is named after him today. Archaeologists think that people started to live in the town of Rome long before Romulus and Remus were alive. However, some people still believe the legend to this day.

In AD 43 the Roman Emperor Claudius invaded Britain. The Romans called Britain Britannia. Claudius sent ships from Gaul (modern France) to invade an area around what is today called Kent. Historians still **debate** what the Romans wanted with Britain. Was it for grain, lead or maybe for gold? Or, did they just want more power and more land for their growing empire? Perhaps the Romans were scared that the Celts who lived in Britain might attack their other land in Gaul.

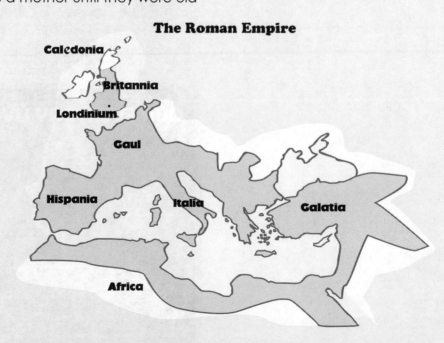

The Roman Empire

Caledonia

Britannia

Londinium

Gaul

Hispania

Italia

Galatia

Africa

COMPARING LIFESTYLES ✱

ACTIVITIES

Since the Roman Empire there have been many great empires in the world. People have been **inspired** by the idea that one town can grow so strong and take over so much land. Celts that lived in Scotland had links with other Celtic tribes that stretched as far south as Spain. Recently, Britain had an even bigger empire. It stretched from Australia to America. It was said that the sun never set on the British Empire. What do you think this means?

a) List three great civilisations of the ancient world.

b) Define the word 'empire'.

c) Define the word 'legend'.

d) Define the word 'colonies'

e) List three possible reasons for the Romans invading Britain.

f) Do you believe the legend of Romulus and Remus? Give a reason for your answer.

Copy and complete the following table which shows Roman place names using the internet or an atlas.

Roman place name	Name of place today
Londinium	
Gaul	
Britannia	
Caledonia	
Hispania	
Italia	
Galatia	

MAKE THE LINK

In **Geography** you could look at the areas of the world the Romans took over. In **Geography** we look at why particular areas of land are important to people.

In **English** we read many stories, some of which are legends. Think about legends. Do you believe in any legends? Are they based on truth and facts? How could you find out what is fact and what is fiction?

In **Personal and Social Education** we look at what motivates people. In the story of Rome many people were inspired by the legend of the boys being brought up by a wolf. What things inspire people today? What sorts of things inspire you?

23

THINK TIME
Think about what motivates you to do well. Some people are motivated to do great things by stories or dreams that other people have told them about.

WHO WERE THE CELTS?

The word Celtic is often used to describe tribes of people who spoke a similar language during the Iron Age (around 700 BC to AD 100). They used the same artwork and designs, which are often represented in knotwork patterns like the one shown. Much of their art was made using iron. Iron was becoming more popular as bronze was running out. Also iron was a much harder metal than bronze. Iron swords were stronger and iron farming tools lasted longer and could plough deeper into the ground.

The Iron Age Celts came from an area near to where Austria is today. The Romans called these people *Celtae*. The Romans kept great records when they invaded Britain. They said there were lots of different Celtic tribes in the north of Britain. The Romans called the north of Britain Caledonia.

The area in which the Celts lived began to grow. Like the Vikings, they began to move to new places. Soon Celtic tribes could be found as far north as Scotland and as far south as Spain. Many Celtic tribes settled in Ireland as well. Today many place names come from Celtic times. For example, the word 'aber' means the mouth of a river or a ford, like Aberdeen. Also, the word 'drum' means a hill and the word 'kil' means church.

Think of places in your area that include aber, drum or kil. Other places to come from Celtic times are Traprain Law near Haddington. This was the site of a major hill fort and the centre of the Votadini. This tribe controlled the Lothian area. The town Clackmannan and Penicuik got their name from Celtic times.

As well as Celtic place names, we also have lots of evidence that archaeologists have found. Wood from Celts' houses was found in Loch Tay. Since then a Celtic house has been rebuilt there.

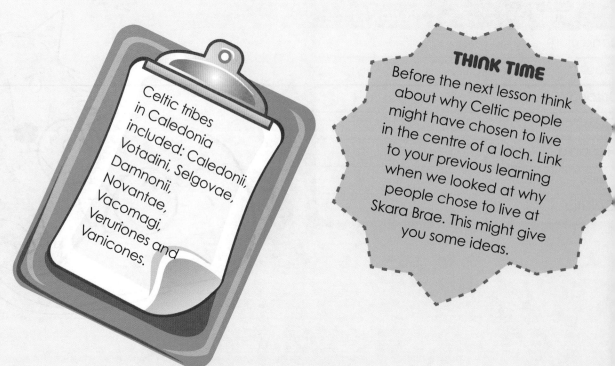

Celtic tribes in Caledonia included: Caledonii, Votadini, Selgovae, Damnonii, Novantae, Vacomagi, Veruriones and Vanicones.

THINK TIME

Before the next lesson think about why Celtic people might have chosen to live in the centre of a loch. Link to your previous learning when we looked at why people chose to live at Skara Brae. This might give you some ideas.

COMPARING LIFESTYLES *

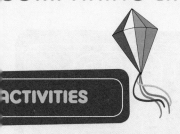

ACTIVITIES

1 Make a list of materials Celtic people used to make tools.

2 Compare the tools Celts were using with the tools used by settlers in Skara Brae.

Which one would be easier to use and why.

3 Make a list of three countries the Celts lived in.

4 Make a list of place names in Scotland which have Celtic origins. You might want to use a map or the internet to help you with this task.

MAKE THE LINK

In **Computing Studies** you could search the internet for the various place names to try to find out which type of Celtic housing can be found in each place. Each place is now a site of archaeological interest. Many tourists visit these places. This is something you will also look at in **Geography**.

In **Craft, Design and Technology** you look at different types of tools and different materials that things are made from. You find out what materials work best for which types of tasks.

DID YOU KNOW?

There is a theme park in Aberdeenshire where you can see what it was like to live in Neolithic Scotland (around the time of the settlers in Skara Brae), Bronze/Iron Age Scotland (during the time of the Celts) and at the time of Roman attacks. The park is open to schools and members of the public.

25

OUR EVERYDAY LIVES:

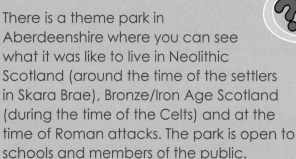

Lots of place names we use today come from various times in history. We have now found out that lots of place names come from times when the Romans and Vikings invaded Scotland and from when the Celts lived in Scotland. My name, Neil, comes from the Gaelic language spoken by some Celts. Neil means champion. What does your name mean and where does it come from?

COMPARING ROMAN AND CELTIC ARMIES

The Romans fought many battles as they expanded their empire. The army was very important to the Romans. Their soldiers were the best organised in the world. The Roman army took over lots of areas of land.

The Roman army was split up into three sections: infantry, cavalry and artillery.

The **infantry** were soldiers that fought on foot. The best soldiers were called legionaries. The legionaries had to swear an oath to be faithful to their emperor, to obey all orders and to never leave a battle unless they were attempting to save another legionary's life. The **cavalry** were soldiers who fought on the backs of horses. Lastly, **artillery** soldiers fired objects long distances at enemies.

The artillery fired two main objects: arrows and large rocks. The Romans got a lot of their ideas about artillery from the Greeks. However, like the Greeks, they did not yet know how to use explosives like gunpowder. Instead, they used complex machines which would fire objects hundreds of metres using a series of tightened ropes.

The armies went into battles with a gold eagle held at the front. Trumpets would be used to help organise and give orders to

the men. While the Romans were a fearsome fighting force, we know they were afraid of Celtic warriors.

The Celts tried to frighten enemies before battles had even begun. They would put lime and chalk in their hair. This made their long hair stick out. Their clothing was dyed bright colours although some would fight naked! Many wore necklaces called torcs. The Celts were very superstitious. They believed that torcs would bring them good luck and protect them in battle. Battles involving Celts were noisy affairs. They would use long trumpets that were made to look like boars' heads. Celtic warriors would run into battle making a loud battle cry.

The Celts had very powerful weapons. Solid, long iron swords were used for cutting and slashing. They also had daggers for close range fighting and spears for throwing. Like the Romans, not all soldiers fought on foot. Many went into battle on two-wheeled chariots pulled by horses. A Celtic chariot was found by archaeologists at Newbridge near Edinburgh. It is believed two people used the chariot. The driver controlled the horses while a warrior threw spears at the enemy.

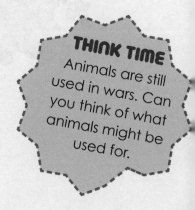

THINK TIME
Animals are still used in wars. Can you think of what animals might be used for.

26

COMPARING LIFESTYLES *

ACTIVITIES

1 Pick out the items a Roman legionary would probably use in battle
- shield
- dagger
- machine gun
- sword (gladius)
- javelin (pilum)
- missile launcher
- radio communication
- helmet

2 Pick out the items a Celtic warrior would probably use in battle
- gold
- necklace
- shield
- iron sword
- pistol
- colourful clothing
- tank
- chariot
- spear
- trumpet

Copy and complete this table from the items you selected for your two warriors.

Items for Defence	Items for Attacking

4 With a partner, discuss which army you think would be more successful – the Roman army or the Celtic army.

5 As a class discuss the differences between warfare in Roman and Celtic times with warfare today.

MAKE THE LINK

Think about the sorts of objects a Roman legionary used. What materials would be needed to make these objects? In **Geography** think about where in the world these materials can be found. In **Craft, Design and Technology** discuss how easy or hard it would be to make some of these objects.

In **Science** we might look at how tension and energy is stored. Look at how the Romans made machines which could propel missiles long distances. They used ropes which were tightly pulled so that they could be fired long distances.

DID YOU KNOW?

The Roman army was very well organised. There were legions which contained around five to six thousand soldiers. During Emperor Augustus' time in charge there were twenty-eight legions! The legion was commanded by a legate. Each legion was divided up into cohorts of five or six hundred men. Within each cohort was a century of around one hundred men, although it was generally found to be only eighty men. The century was commanded by a centurion.

27

OUR EVERYDAY LIVES:

Today many organisations are based on similar structures to those of the Roman army. Think about how many people you know really well. You may have over a hundred Facebook or Bebo friends but how many do you know really well? Make a list and see how many people you could command at one time.

WHO WERE THE MOST EFFECTIVE WARRIORS?

In the last lesson we learned that the Romans were afraid of a group of people called the Celts. Some Celts fought against the Romans in Wales and also in France. The Celts were very difficult for the Romans to beat even though the Romans were well equipped and had lots of legionaries. The Romans invaded Britain in AD 43. There were some revolts against the Romans. One was led by a female war leader called Bouddica in AD 61. In AD 78 a new person was sent to rule Britain. The southern part of Britain was living at peace with the Romans by the time Julius Agricola took over. Romans and Britons traded with each other and lived beside each other. Britons paid taxes to the Romans and some Britons even joined into the Roman army.

The Romans wanted to control Caledonia. Many people living in northern Caledonia painted their faces. The Romans called them Picts (or painted people). The Celts who came from this area caused the Romans a lot of problems. The Romans built two walls to stop Celtic attacks.

In AD 79 Agricola attacked northern Britain. A famous battle took place called Mons Graupius although historians are not sure where this took place. At this battle the Celts were commanded by Calgacus or **Galgach**. His name was Celtic for swordsman.

Roman Soldier

The climate here is miserable with lots of rain and mist. People living in Caledonia have red hair and massive limbs. They have large swords and some even have chariots.

Celt

The enemy is rich and also greedy. Women are seduced by Romans. Men are taxed and made into slaves. But the Romans are not from here. They have no wives to inspire them, no parents to taunt them if they run away. We fight for our ancestors and descendants.

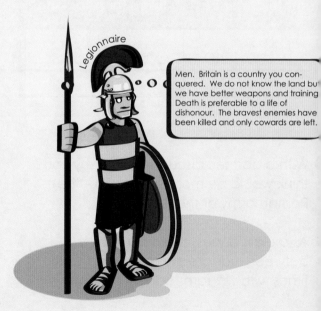

Legionnaire

Men. Britain is a country you conquered. We do not know the land but we have better weapons and training. Death is preferable to a life of dishonour. The bravest enemies have been killed and only cowards are left.

28

WHO WERE THE MOST EFFECTIVE WARRIORS?

Battle of Mons Graupius

The Celts were double the size of the Roman army. Their chariots made them quicker and far more mobile. The chariots also gave them some protection. The Roman army had fewer men but was better organised and had far better training.

In the battle the Celts lost lots of men. The roman writer Tacitus said that the Celts cried out when carrying their wounded men off the battlefields. Tacitus also accused the Picts of taking out their frustration with violence against their own women and children. However, this might be biased.

What we do know is that Agricola was called back by Rome to defend another area in the empire. Even though the Romans killed more Celts, the Romans never attacked northern Britain again.

In AD 122 the Romans built Hadrian's Wall in the north of England to stop attacks from Caledonia. Later, in AD 142, they built the Antonine Wall from the River Forth to the River Clyde. Parts of the walls and forts can still be seen today.

ACTIVITIES

1 When did the Romans first invade Britain?

2 When did the Romans attack northern Britain?

3 What evidence is there that Romans and Britons got on well with each other?

4 What evidence is there that the Romans were not popular with all Britons?

5 Do you think Tacitus' account of the battle of Mons Graupius will be useful? Might it be biased? Give a reason for your answers.

6 Which of the speeches on the other page would inspire you to fight? Give a reason for your answer.

7 Write a newspaper report on the Battle of Mons Graupius. It can be from either the Roman or Celtic point of view. It should contain the following:

- Name of newspaper
- Date
- Appropriate short catchy headline
- Well written story
- Interviews

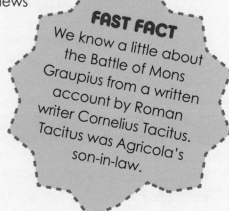

FAST FACT
We know a little about the Battle of Mons Graupius from a written account by Roman writer Cornelius Tacitus. Tacitus was Agricola's son-in-law.

COMPARING ROMAN AND CELTIC HOUSING

Romans must have found Caledonia a very different place from Rome and the other warmer places that Roman soldiers came from. Houses in Rome would have been very different to the house a Celt lived in. Celtic houses were made from wood, mud, grass and straw. The main aim of celtic houses was to protect those living inside from the weather and from possible attack. They were kept warm by the heat from animals that lived in the same houses. Celts lived in three different types of houses.

Brochs/duns: these were large stone towers. There were no windows. It would have been very dark but also very safe.

Crannogs: these were built in lochs and rivers. Wooden stilts kept the house clear of the water. The wooden walkway to the house could be removed so that enemies and wild animals could not get near the house. Living on water also meant there was more space on the land to farm.

Hill forts: some villages were built on top of hills for protection. They were then surrounded by steep walls. The remains of one such fort at White Caterthun in Angus can still be seen today. Where the wall once stood is marked on the ground.

Roman housing was very different, depending on whether you were rich or poor. There is little evidence of differences between rich Celts' houses and the houses of others. However, rich Romans lived in grand **villas**. They had many rooms, including reception rooms, bedrooms, libraries, store rooms and large kitchens where the servants would prepare food. Many of the floors

and walls were made from marble. Under the floors hot air would flow around like a modern central heating system.

Poorer people lived in **flats or apartments**. These were not as luxurious as villas and were built from poor quality materials. Sometimes they were over five storeys tall and were overcrowded. On occasion they collapsed or caught fire.

Roman soldiers lived in **forts**. Roman engineers were very skilled at building these massive structures. They were well defended with high wooden walls. If they were staying for longer, stone walls would be constructed. Inside the fort there were many buildings: armouries stored weapons, offices were built for commanders. Large buildings housed soldiers, workers and horses. Of course, it would not be Roman without a bath-house! Bath-houses were used for cleaning but also for socialising. They were used as meeting places and many business deals were made there.

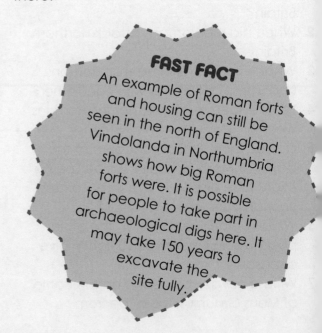

FAST FACT

An example of Roman forts and housing can still be seen in the north of England. Vindolanda in Northumbria shows how big Roman forts were. It is possible for people to take part in archaeological digs here. It may take 150 years to excavate the site fully.

COMPARING LIFESTYLES *

ACTIVITIES

Make a list of three types of Celtic housing.

2 Make a list of three types of Roman housing.

3 Discuss with a partner which Roman house you would like to stay in and give a reason for your answer.

4 Discuss with a partner which Celtic house you would not like to live in and give a reason for your answer.

ENTERPRISE ACTIVITY

Make a model of a Roman house and a Celtic house. To make the task more realistic and challenging, make the models only out of materials you find in your school playground. The Romans and Celts only used materials around them so you should be able to do the same!

Once you have built your two models make an information sheet showing how people lived in each type of house. Your information sheet should come to a conclusion as to which type of housing you would prefer to live in and why.

Invite other people to come and see your models. Give a short presentation on the models you have made and explain how they are different from the living conditions we experience today.

MAKE THE LINK

In **Geography** we often look at travel and tourism. Think about places in the world you would want to go and places that you would not want to go. It is quite clear that living in Britain was not the first choice for many Roman soldiers. The climate put many of them off, as did the fierce fighting.

In **Craft, Design and Technology** look at the sorts of tools that are needed to build a house. Roman engineers used many tools that we still use today. Look in your technology department to see if you can find a tri-square, a plumb line and an early version of a spirit measure called a chorobates. Find out what each item is used for. To make sure the buildings had straight lines and right angled corners, Roman surveyors used a groma. Find out what surveyors use today to do the same job.

DID YOU KNOW?

The first writing in British history was found at Vindolada. Letters found there are to and from people living in the Roman fort there. The earliest writing found is from a wife to her soldier husband. She was writing about socks!

OUR EVERYDAY LIVES:

Constructing houses today uses many of the skills and tools that were used in Roman times. Building sites have many jobs available on them. Site managers and surveyors oversee the work being done. Other workers are required such as plasterers, builders, roofers and glaziers. Many of these jobs existed in Roman times.

COMPARING RELIGION AND BELIEFS

Today many people in our society believe in religion but do not belong to a church. For example, they will get married in a church but would not go to a church on a regular basis. This was very different at the time of the Celts and Romans. Both societies were serious in their beliefs. Their beliefs were also very different.

The Romans worshipped many different gods and goddesses. Some gods were extremely important such as Jupiter. Romans believed that Jupiter ruled over all the gods and goddesses. People feared he would strike

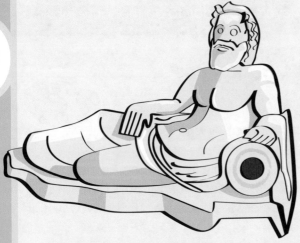

them with a thunderbolt if he was not happy. Neptune was the god of the sea and Mars was the god of war. Statues of gods could be found in town centres. Many families kept small altars of gods in their homes. People prayed to the gods and made sacrifices for them. Up until Emperor Augustus' time, human sacrifices still happened. Later, only animals were offered as sacrifices to the gods. At harvest time gods were thanked during large festivals.

Some rulers were made into gods when they died. Romans were very superstitious and even Julius Caesar saw fortune-tellers. One foresaw his death before Caesar was murdered!

Celts were also very superstitious. Stones were erected to Celtic gods and these are thought to have been the centre of religious ceremonies. Celts were pagan and worshipped the gods of earth, sun, moon and woods. They sometimes gave them offerings of wine and water. Important tools, jewellery and weapons were also sacrificed.

Hundreds of items found in Duddingston Loch in Edinburgh are believed to have been sacrificed. Human sacrifices also occurred and were carried out by Druids. The Druids were highly respected men in Celtic communities. The Lindow Man was an example of a human sacrifice. His body was found in a bog and is believed to be the remains of someone who was sacrificed to the gods.

Both Romans and Celts were eventually converted to Christianity. Jesus Christ had been crucified by the Romans and his message began to spread around the world. Christ's religion, Christianity, spread to Caledonia from people living close to Hadrian's Wall. Also, a missionary called Columba came from Ireland to spread the Christian message. Many Christian crosses can be found across Scotland, decorated with Celtic art. Slowly people converted to Christianity.

32

COMPARING LIFESTYLES *

ACTIVITIES

Look at the table below and decide if the gods are Roman or Celtic. Tick the correct column.

God	Roman	Celtic
Sun		
Mars		
Earth		
Jupiter		
Neptune		

Make a list of items people would sacrifice to the gods.

Design a statue to a Roman god. Choose one from the list above. What do you think this god would look like? What did Romans make the god look like when they made their statues?

Look at the table below which shows how people might find out about a new religion in the past and today. Tick the correct boxes in the table. The first one is done for you.

How people find out information	Then	Now
Internet		✓
Word of mouth		
Newspapers		
News on the TV		

MAKE THE LINK

In **Art** we look at designs and patterns. Look closely at Celtic designs and Celtic art to see how they are formed. Ask your teacher to show you illustrations from the Book of Kells.

In **Enterprise** or **Business Education** think about some of the jewellery and other objects that are made and sold using Celtic designs. Could you make a Celtic product and attempt to sell it?

In **Religious Education** look at the origins of Christianity and of other world religions. How are religions formed and how do they become popular?

DID YOU KNOW?

One of the most important primary sources from this time is stored at Trinity College in Dublin, Ireland. The Book of Kells was made by Celts who had converted to Christianity. It contains some gospels from the Bible and is colourfully and carefully decorated with Celtic art. Today, many visitors queue to see the book every day. The book was moved from Iona to Ireland in a hurry. When the Vikings invaded Scotland they took lots of gold and silver from religious places. The monks at Iona moved the Book of Kells to Ireland so that it would be safe.

33

OUR EVERYDAY LIVES:

Religion and beliefs play a vital role in lots of people's lives. In Scotland today people celebrate and worship a variety of different religions.

WHAT DID THE ROMANS DO FOR US?

Despite never conquering Scotland the Romans still have a huge influence on our lives today. During their time in the south of Britain they left behind lots of new inventions, ideas and ways of living. Look at the various achievements of the Romans. Which ones are still important today?

The Romans were very famous for building straight roads. Many of the main roads across Britain today follow the Roman roads from centuries before.

Today we use the Roman calendar which was introduced by Julius Caesar. The months in the calendar are named after Roman gods.

Roman houses had early plumbing systems using water in their homes. We have similar systems today.

The Romans made many advances

in medicines using plants and oils. They also made surgical tools very similar to ones we use today.

The Latin language and alphabet we use today is very much based on the language the Romans used.

Every ten years we take a census. A census i a count of the number of people living in the country. The Romans used to take a census so that they knew how many people were in the empire.

Lots of our buildings followed Roman design with arches and carved columns. Are there any in your area?

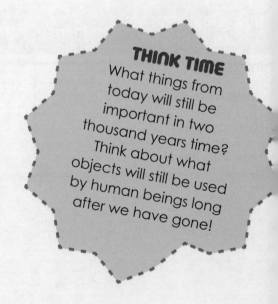

THINK TIME
What things from today will still be important in two thousand years time? Think about what objects will still be used by human beings long after we have gone!

34

COMPARING LIFESTYLES *

ACTIVITIES

1 Make a list of four things the Romans did for us.

2 With a partner decide which of the four things is the most important and give a reason for your answer.

3 Compare your answer with others in your class. Did you all decide on the same thing? If not, can you persuade the others to change their minds?

MAKE THE LINK

In **Maths** look at how the Romans contributed to our understanding of numbers. For example, a century means one hundred, as in one hundred soldiers. Find out what other maths words there are and where they come from. How many of the words we use come from Roman times?

In **Craft, Design and Technology** we could look at the number of building and engineering tools which were used or invented in Roman times.

In **Modern Studies** we look at how countries are ruled. We may look at Republics where Presidents rule the country, just like the Roman Republic. Is Britain ruled the same way?

DID YOU KNOW?

35

In AD 180 a Roman force was sent deep into Caledonia. The IX (9th) legion was said to have disappeared. Books were written afterwards trying to explain how the Roman soldiers mysteriously disappeared. Some said they were killed by the Celts. However, historians now believe they retreated south of Hadrian's Wall and were sent to fight somewhere else in the Roman Empire.

OUR EVERYDAY LIVES:

Roman life was a mix of work and leisure time. Romans always found time for various games and social activities. At the centre of Roman social life was the bath-house. Other entertainment involved seeing chariot races and gladiator shows.

A GOOD KING?

3200 BC	79 AD	795 AD	1286 AD	1305 AD	1314 AD	today
Settlers at Skara Brae	Romans attack Britain	Viking attacks	Alexander III dies	William Wallace dies	Bruce wins at Bannokburn	

When the Romans left Britain, Scotland was still a divided country. Lots of different groups of people lived in the country. Picts, Britons, Angles and Gaels all lived in Scotland. They each controlled a bit of land in what we today call Scotland.

The Picts became the strongest group. They beat off many Viking attacks. Some believe a Pict called Kenneth MacAlpin became the first king of a united Scotland in 843. MacAlpin defeated the Angles but the Gaels were still separate. In 899 Donald II became King of Alba. He was followed by Constantine II. Both were truly kings of a united Scotland. Scotland had difficult relations with their southern neighbours, Angleland or, as we know it, England.

Under the kingship of Alexander III (1249–86), things seemed to improve. He was an excellent king. When Alexander III was in charge Scotland became friends with England once again. The countries began to trade goods, such as wool. The reign of Alexander III became known as 'the Golden Age of Scotland' as there were no wars with England. Things were so good that Alexander even married an English princess, Margaret. Alexander III's only war was with Norwegian kings. The Norwegians gave up their claim to the Hebrides and Alexander gained more land for Scotland. However, things began to go wrong for Alexander III and eventually for Scotland. His wife, Margaret, died. Then his oldest child Alexander died in 1284 and his middle child David also died. His youngest child had moved to Norway to marry Erik of Norway. Sadly she also died.

Alexander remarried. On a stormy night in March 1286 Alexander's new wife, Yolande, was in Kinghorn in Fife. The king was in Edinburgh Castle and wanted to see his wife. His bodyguards told him that it was too windy and wet to travel and that he should wait until the morning. However, the king got his way. He crossed the Firth of Forth from Edinburgh to Fife. The ferryman again warned him not to go. At Inverkeithing in Fife someone offered him shelter for the night. The king was determined to go on. As he continued along the cliff edge on horseback he lost two of his guides in the darkness. The next time the king was seen was the following morning. He lay at the bottom of the cliffs with his horse. The king was dead.

FAST FACT

From 1214 Scotland was ruled by a warrior king. Alexander II united Scotland. He crushed revolts in the Highlands. He also attacked England and got as far as Dover. He died in 1249. Relations were not good with England during his reign.

36

PEOPLE AND EVENTS

ACTIVITIES

1 Make a list all the Scottish kings you have read about on the opposite page.

2 Write a fact about each one.

3 Explain how you can tell Scotland and England got on well during the reign of Alexander III.

4 Produce a family tree for Alexander III's closest family. Remember, the oldest person always goes to the left.

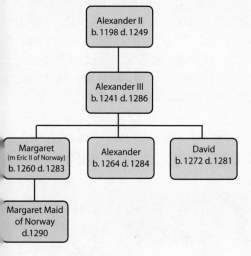

Alexander II
b. 1198 d. 1249

Alexander III
b. 1241 d. 1286

Margaret
(m Eric II of Norway)
b. 1260 d. 1283

Alexander
b. 1264 d. 1284

David
b. 1272 d. 1281

Margaret Maid
of Norway
d.1290

AND NOW TRY

Write a newspaper report describing the death of Alexander III. It should have the following things in it:

- Name of newspaper
- Date
- Appropriate short catchy headline
- Well written story
- Interviews
- Appropriate picture (s)

PEOPLE AND EVENTS IN THE MAKING OF SCOTLAND

MAKE THE LINK

In **English** we look at how to write reports in an interesting and informative way. We think about the way we describe the events so that the reader is clear what has happened.

In **Geography** we look at weather and how extreme weather can have an impact on human behaviour. In 1286 there were no weather forecasts.

In both **Science** and **Geography** we could find out how to make weather instruments from basic materials. Could these have been made during Alexander III's time to help warn the king on that fateful night?

DID YOU KNOW?

The English writer William Shakespeare wrote many plays, some about kings and queens. One of his most famous plays was about the Scottish king, Macbeth. He ruled between 1040 and 1057. The play described the period when he was an army commander during King Duncan's rule of Scotland.

OUR EVERYDAY LIVES

In the thirteenth century Scotland was ruled by a monarch (a king or a queen). Scotland and England were separate countries and each had their own monarch. Today Scotland and England are one country. While we have a monarch, they alone do not rule. We also vote for a Prime Minister. Do you know who the monarch is today? Do you know who the Prime Minister is today?

DEATH AND DISASTER

Scotland was in turmoil when people heard the news of the death of their beloved king. With no male heir to the throne this was a major disaster. However, Alexander III had a granddaughter living in Norway. Can you remember why Alexander's granddaughter, Margaret, was in Norway?

FAST FACT
The word 'heir' means successor, or the next in line to the throne. Normally the crown is passed to the oldest male in the family tree. Can you remember which side the oldest child appears on the family tree?

Until that time important men called the Guardians would look after Scotland. They made one huge decision. They agreed that the young princess should be married to the English king's son. A marriage between Margaret of Scotland and Edward I's son, Edward, would be a major event at this time. It might keep Scotland and England from fighting each other.

Margaret began the long and stormy dangerous voyage from Norway in 1290. Sadly, she would not make it for the proposed wedding. The boat carrying her had to stop at Orkney as she fell ill. She did not recover and died soon after being taken ashore. This was the second crisis to face Scotland. The second crisis was more serious. Who would rule Scotland now?

Margaret Maid of Norway had no children. There was no obvious heir to the throne.

To some, Margaret Maid of Norway seemed to be the ideal solution to Scotland's problems. However, not everyone was happy with this solution. First, Margaret was female so did not meet the stereotypical image of a monarch at that time. The people wanted a strong man who could lead the nation and could be a warrior king if battles took place. Also, Margaret was only a young girl. She was unable to look after herself, far less become the next ruler of Scotland. Lastly, Margaret lived in Norway and she would need to be brought to Scotland.

PEOPLE AND EVENTS

ACTIVITIES

1. Make a list of reasons why people in Scotland were concerned about Margaret Maid of Norway becoming Scotland's next monarch.

2. Describe the death of Margaret Maid of Norway.

3. Explain why the death of Margaret Maid of Norway created a major problem for Scotland.

AND NOW TRY

4. With a partner, compare the role and treatment of women in Middle Ages Scotland with today. What sort of roles do you think women were responsible for in the Middle Ages? How and why do you think women's position changed?

Complete the following table for Scotland's two disaster:

Police report		
Victim	Alexander III	Maid Margaret
Date of incident		
Possible witnesses		
Position of body		
Cause of death		
Impact of death in Scotland		
Probable circumstances		

PEOPLE AND EVENTS IN THE MAKING OF SCOTLAND

MAKE THE LINK

In **Science** you will look at medical care and how ill people are cared for. Illnesses that killed people many years ago are easily cured today. Many medical improvements are as a result of Scottish inventors, scientists and doctors like Elsie Inglis, James Young Simpson and Alexander Fleming. In **Technology** and in **History** you might look at how transport and travel has changed over time. Again, Scots were heavily involved in the transport revolution. Scots pioneered the steam engine John Boyd Dunlop, pioneered the pneumatic tyre.

In **Modern Studies** you will find out about how changes in leaders and governments can have a dramatic effect.

In **Personal and Social Education** you may want to discuss the position of women in our communities today.

DID YOU KNOW?

Orkney has a long and interesting maritime history.
Not only did Margaret land there but many other events happened there. At the end of the First World War the German navy was forced to scuttle their fleet at Scapa Flow. Also, one of the biggest disasters in Royal Navy history happened there. Find out more in chapter 7.

OUR EVERYDAY LIVES

Police today investigate accidents. When an accident occurs some of the best evidence comes from eyewitnesses. Eyewitnesses can be useful because they saw what happened but usually they only see things from one point of view. The best police investigations rely on lots of pieces of evidence. What other evidence do police gather at crime/accident scenes today?

EDWARD'S CHOICE

After Margaret died Scotland had to quickly find a King or a Queen. It may seem strange but the Scottish Guardians decided to ask King Edward of England to come to Scotland to help choose the next ruler. This had to be done quickly because powerful people in Scotland were gathering armies. People in Scotland were about to fight each other to try to win the crown of Scotland.

TOP TIP
A civil war is when two groups of people from the same country fight each other. Find out where else in the world there have been civil wars.

Edward was maybe not such a bad person to decide after all! He was a king himself so would know what the job required and would know who was best to do it. He was also Scotland's nearest monarch and relations

had been good between Scotland and England for some time. Furthermore, Edward was seen as a good king by others because of his good leadership in England and also because he was a Christian king. This was at a time when the Christian countries fought against Muslim countries in a set of wars called the Crusades. Scotland was deeply religious and Edward's record of being in these wars gained him respect in Scotland.

Lots of people told Edward that they should be king of Scotland. Edward had thirteen possible candidates. However, only four had strong links to the Scottish Royal family. Edward is thinking which one to choose in the picture below.

Edward chose John Balliol. He chose Balliol for two reasons. First, Balliol's position in the Scottish royal family tree meant that he had a strong claim to be the next king. Also, he was very weak and Edward wanted a weak king in Scotland. Edward wanted to be able to push Balliol around and bully him. It seemed that things were only going to get worse for Scotland!

40

Robert the Bruce

John Balliol

William of Hastings

John Comyn

PEOPLE AND EVENTS

ACTIVITIES

1. Make a list of reasons why Edward of England was asked to help choose Scotland's next king.

2. Imagine you were choosing a king for Scotland. Make a list of strengths and skills the new king would need to have.

3. Imagine you are John Balliol. Write a letter to the people of Scotland telling them that the country is now safe. Also, tell them what sort of things you plan to do as king:

PEOPLE AND EVENTS IN THE MAKING OF SCOTLAND

MAKE THE LINK

Most schools now have **student councils**. Think about how candidates are selected and are voted onto student councils. Do you think about what skills representatives need? In **Religious Education** you may want to investigate the Crusades further. In history different religious groups have fought with each other. Why do differences lead to conflicts? In **Personal and Social Education** you look at bullying and ways to stop bullying. In **Modern Studies** look at decisions making are made in different countries. Is it better if lots of people get the right to vote or is it better if one person makes the decision? If one person makes all the decisions this is called a dictatorship. Why do we have different systems of decision making in different countries?

41

DID YOU KNOW?

All Scottish kings were crowned on the Stone of Destiny in Scone, Perthshire. It was a Gaelic tradition that became Scottish tradition. The first Scottish king to be crowned at Scone on the Stone of Destiny was Constantine II in AD 900. He defeated Viking invaders in 904.

OUR EVERYDAY LIVES:

Every day politicians are in the news about decisions that they have or have not made. We live in a country where we can choose who runs our country by voting. In our story Edward has made the decision for the Scottish people. Today, that would not be the case. We even have our own Scottish Parliament to make decisions for Scotland. You will find out more about the Scottish Parliament in chapter 5.

EXIT JOHN BALLIOL ... ENTER WILLIAM WALLACE

Do you remember in the last section you wrote a letter from Balliol telling the Scottish people all the brilliant things you were going to do during your time as king? Well, John Balliol was probably thinking exactly the same and was planning to do lots of good things for Scotland. However, Balliol never got a chance to do very much because Edward wanted to control Scotland and its new king.

Edward soon began to take away Scotland's freedom and aimed to end its independence. Edward had asked John to send Scottish troops to fight in an English war against France. Balliol refused to do this. Edward was furious and attacked Scotland.

First he destroyed the town of Berwick, killing the people who lived there. Next he took John Balliol's royal robes from him. This was very embarrassing for King John and got him the nickname Toom Tabard (Empty Jacket). He stole Edward Balliol's Crown Jewels and the Stone of Destiny and took all of Scotland's taxes. Then he appointed his friend as the Governor of Scotland.

All important Scots were forced to swear allegiance to Edward by signing the Ragman's Roll. Eventually, Balliol had to leave Scotland and was exiled in France. Although he later got the chance to return, it would never be safe to do so. He lived the rest of his life in France. He was a king without a throne or a crown. Edward was in charge.

42

Case study: William Wallace

William Wallace lived in the west of Scotland. He had refused to sign the Ragman's Roll. His wife or a friend's wife (we don't know for sure) had been killed by English soldiers who occupied Scotland. Wallace took his revenge. He killed the man in charge of English soldiers in his area. The killing of this man, William Hazelrigg, the Sheriff of Lanark, was the first time Scotland had hit back.

Wallace was now a wanted man. However, he quickly gained support from Scottish people and gathered an army. They had fewer soldiers and were poorly armed. Scots soldiers made spears and used farming tools as weapons. Some of the richer soldiers owned swords. On the other hand, the English army were very well equipped. Their soldiers had swords, wooden shields, heavy armour and helmets.

THINK TIME

Independence is something that lots of countries fight for. Often, countries are taken over by people from another country. Can you think of any examples of this?

PEOPLE AND EVENTS

ACTIVITIES

1. Make a list of all the things Edward did to Scotland.

2. With a partner, decide which thing on your list hurt Scotland the most. Be able to give a reason for your decision.

3. Write a letter telling kings in other countries what Edward has done to Scotland. Try to persuade them to help Scotland.

4. Compare the Scottish and English armies.

5. Make a WANTED poster for William Wallace. It should show two things he is wanted for.

   Remember, there are no primary source pictures of Wallace. Any picture of him shows what an artist thinks he looks like. What do you think he looks like?

6. Think of ten questions which you would ask William Wallace if you could interview him.

PEOPLE AND EVENTS IN THE MAKING OF SCOTLAND

MAKE THE LINK

Ask your librarian how to find out more information on William Wallace. The internet may provide some answers but your librarian will be able to show you what your school library or learning resource centre has. You should use books, encyclopaedias and the internet.

In **Craft, Design and Technology** we look at different types of materials and how easy they are to make items from. Think about the different types of weapons used by the Scottish and the English armies.

In **Home Economics,** think about foods found in the countryside. Wallace's army had to live off the land. How would you make enough food for an army? In **Hospitality** you might look at how companies cater for lots of people.

DID YOU KNOW?

43

You can now see the Stone of Destiny and the Crown Jewels in Edinburgh Castle. Both were returned to Scotland in 1996. Some say that it may not be the real Stone of Destiny. On Christmas Day 1950 a group of Scottish students stole the stone from Westminster in London. They later returned it to the police but some say it was a fake that they gave back!

OUR EVERYDAY LIVES

Edward had tried to take away Scotland's independence and freedom. He was nicknamed 'the Hammer of the Scots'. This has happened many times in history when one ruler tries to take over another country. In the 1930s Adolf Hitler took over large parts of Europe. He also persecuted Jewish people. We learn about history so that we can try to prevent events like this happening again in the future.

WALLACE WINS

In the last section you explained why Wallace could not fight big battles. Wallace had to put his small number of soldier and weapons to good use. He had to carefully devise a plan and tactics.

Wallace decided to use special tactics to beat the large English army. In September 1297, he gathered his army around Stirling Bridge. He knew the English army would have to cross the river there. His men were armed with long spears which they had made themselves from wood. Some of the spears were over two metres long. The men watched the English cross the bridge from a nearby hill. Then Wallace got his men to use the spears to defeat the English cavalry.

The English cavalry crossed the bridge and were killed as Wallace's men rushed down from the hill. The bridge could only take two horses side by side at any one time. English soldiers at the other side of the bridge could not see the Scottish soldiers attacking their friends so kept on sending more and more horses onto the bridge. English soldiers that reached the other side were soon killed. Some tried to retreat but could not because the bridge was so crowded. Men started to jump over the bridge into the river. They drowned in their heavy armour. Scotland had won its first major victory.

Jubilant Scots soldiers found King Edward's treasurer for Scotland. Hugh de Cressingham had taken taxes from Scottish people. The Scots soldiers flayed Cressingham of his skin. Part of his skin was used to make a belt to hold William Wallace's sword. The day was not a complete success for Scotland though Wallace lost one of his best soldiers in the fighting. The loss of Andrew Moray greatly affected Wallace in his next battle...

44

THINK TIME
When we think of heroes/heroines we often think about footballers or pop stars. Think: what qualities do real heroes have?

PEOPLE AND EVENTS

ACTIVITIES

Make a list of the problems that William Wallace faced.

Make a list of reasons why William Wallace won at Stirling Bridge.

■ Many pictures have been drawn through time showing Wallace's victory at Stirling Bridge. Draw your own picture showing William Wallace's victory.

■ Explain why the battle of Stirling Bridge was not a complete success for William Wallace.

AND NOW TRY

Work in pairs. Describe the Battle of Stirling Bridge from the point of view of a Scottish soldier. Then get your partner to describe the Battle of Stirling Bridge from the point of view of an English soldier.

MAKE THE LINK

In **PE** we study how sports managers come up with a strategy and tactics. Managers assess the strengths of their team and the weaknesses in the opposition. Wallace had a long-term strategy. For each battle he also had specific tactics.

In **Geography** we learn how to use maps and look at how humans use different areas of land. Wallace had to look at the land around Stirling and decide what the English army would do. His knowledge of the land meant that he was at a great advantage over his enemies.

In **Art** we look at images of events that happened in the past. Do people add in extra bits or exaggerate what happened? How does this affect our understanding of events in history?

DID YOU KNOW?

Today there is a huge monument in memory of William Wallace. It stands on the hill where Wallace's men hid before the Battle of Stirling Bridge. The monument was constructed in the 1860s. It stands at 67 metres and you can climb all 246 steps inside it.

OUR EVERYDAY LIVES

Architects and engineers use their skills in CDT, maths and physics when they are building bridges, buildings and other structures. Planners have to think about how many people are going to use a structure such as a bridge and the weight it will need to hold.

WALLACE DEFEATED

Many Scottish people think of William Wallace as a hero but this is just an opinion. To many English people, Wallace was a terrorist. This is also an opinion. Wallace led a raid into England and killed innocent English men and women. Some people said he made them dance naked in front of his soldiers before he killed them.

Wallace next fought the English at the Battle of Falkirk in 1298. At Falkirk Wallace planned to use schiltrons. All the soldiers would stand in a circle holding their spears outward. It looked like a giant hedgehog. However, this time Wallace had no bridge. He could not trick the English like he had done before. At Falkirk Edward I had a special weapon – the longbow. It could fire arrows hundreds of metres. It was deadly to the Scots as they had little protection from the arrows that flew through the air at them. Before Wallace could use the schiltron many Scots had already died.

This time Wallace had cavalry of his own. After his earlier victory at Stirling, Wallace had become very popular in Scotland. He had been made the Guardian of Scotland. Many of the rich Scottish landowners, the nobles, now supported him. This was important as many of them owned horses. These could prove useful in a battle. However, when the nobles saw lots of Scots being killed by the longbows they fled the battlefield. Some historians think the nobles deserted Wallace. Others think that they simply ran away so that they could fight the English another day.

Falkirk was a major defeat for Wallace. Wallace went into hiding. He moved between hiding places and caves in the Selkirk Forest. He even gave up his position as Guardian of Scotland. During this time Wallace showed himself to be much more than just a warrior. He wrote letters to the German towns of Lübeck and Hamburg asking them to trade with Scotland.

Wallace was eventually captured by the English. A fellow Scotsman, Sir John Menteith, betrayed him to the English in 1305. Menteith had fought for Scotland but had been taken prisoner himself and was held in England. Here he changed sides. He handed Wallace over to Edward for a bag of gold.

Wallace was taken to London and put on trial. He had no right to speak and there was no jury. He was accused of treason. He said he could not be a traitor to Edward because John Balliol was his king. This argument did not work and Wallace was found guilty. He was hanged, drawn and quartered. While his death was a major blow to Scotland's fight for freedom, it inspired others to take up Scotland's fight for independence.

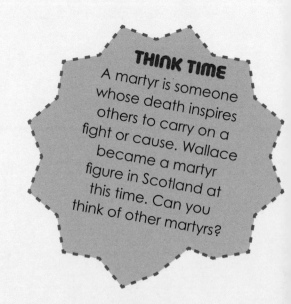

THINK TIME
A martyr is someone whose death inspires others to carry on a fight or cause. Wallace became a martyr figure in Scotland at this time. Can you think of other martyrs?

PEOPLE AND EVENTS

ACTIVITIES

1 Make a list of all the things that show Wallace was a success and all the things that show he was not a failure.

Wallace a success	Wallace not a failure

2 Explain why the trial of William Wallace was not a fair one. Make a list with the other people in your group.

3 Write a newspaper report telling readers about the trial and the execution of William Wallace. It should have the following things in it:

- Name of newspaper
- Date
- Appropriate short catchy headline
- Well written story
- Interviews
- Appropriate picture(s)

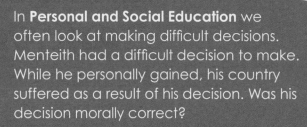

MAKE THE LINK

In **Personal and Social Education** we often look at making difficult decisions. Menteith had a difficult decision to make. While he personally gained, his country suffered as a result of his decision. Was his decision morally correct?

In **Modern Studies** we also look at themes of fairness. We might look at the law and courts to see if they are fair. How have things changed since Wallace's time? Are things fairer today?

Many songs have been written about the Scottish Wars of Independence. In **Music** we might listen to them.

DID YOU KNOW?

47

Wallace's body was cut into various pieces after his execution. These parts were displayed across the country to serve as a warning to others. His head was displayed on a spike on London Bridge. Meanwhile, the other parts of his body were sent to Newcastle, Berwick, Perth and Stirling. The parts of his body were displayed in places where all could see them.

OUR EVERYDAY LIVES

The court and justice system today has got lots of rules to make sure that court cases are fair. A judge ensures court cases are fairly conducted. A jury will decide on the final verdict. In Scots law there are three possible verdicts. If you are accused of a crime you can be found guilty, not guilty or not proven. Not proven means that there is not enough evidence to find the accused person guilty.

BRUCE: THE REAL BRAVEHEART?

In 1995 William Wallace was the main character in a Hollywood blockbuster movie called *Braveheart*. However, some believe it was Robert the Bruce who was the real Braveheart. Robert the Bruce enters our story in a rather peculiar way. We heard about the Bruce family earlier in this chapter when Robert the Bruce wanted Edward to pick him as king after Alexander III's and Margaret's deaths. Edward did not choose Robert the Bruce. Many years later his grandson, Robert the Bruce, also wanted to be king. Robert the Bruce would do anything to become king. He had even fought alongside King Edward at the Battle of Falkirk in 1298!

In 1306, a year after Wallace's death, Robert the Bruce met with John Comyn to discuss who should rule Scotland. Remember Balliol was still in France. No one really knows what happened that night at Greyfriars Church in Dumfries. All we do know is that Bruce left the church and John Comyn lay dead inside. This was a serious crime. Scotland was a deeply religious country since Columba had brought Christianity to Scotland. Committing a crime in a church was very serious. Bruce was now guilty of a crime called of **sacrilege**. This was commiting a crime in a Church. It made him very unpopular with the head of the church at that time, the Pope.

Despite this, Bruce made his way to Scone. Here he gathered with a few close friends and crowned himself king of Scotland. He became a wanted man. Bruce went into hiding because English troops hunted for him, as did the angry Comyn and Balliol families. Bruce's supporters were killed and his sister was hung in a cage outside one of Edward's castles. Edward did the same to

Isabella of Buchan, because she had put the crown on Bruce's head.

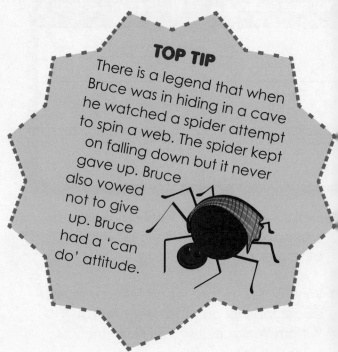

TOP TIP
There is a legend that when Bruce was in hiding in a cave he watched a spider attempt to spin a web. The spider kept on falling down but it never gave up. Bruce also vowed not to give up. Bruce had a 'can do' attitude.

Bruce emerged from this period in fighting mood and started a secret war. He used tactics similar to those of Wallace. Bruce used clever tactics to capture four castles from English soldiers.

He disguised his men as sheep and cattle to retake Roxburgh Castle. He then took Linlithgow by hiding men in straw carts that were taking supplies to the English held castle. Perth Castle was taken by Bruce himself. He waded through a cold moat late at night and then climbed the walls with his men. Lastly, Edinburgh Castle was retaken by Bruce's friend, Sir James Douglas. He used a secret path known to one of the castle workers. Scots soldiers used the path to creep up on English guards and recapture the castle.

48

PEOPLE AND EVENTS

ACTIVITIES

Explain why Bruce was so worried when he sat in the cave and watched the spider. With a partner make a list of things Bruce was worried about.

Match up the following castles with the correct description of how Bruce recaptured them:

Linlithgow	Hid as sheep
Edinburgh	Crossed moat at night
Perth	Used secret path
Roxburgh	Hid in straw carts

MAKE THE LINK

In **Maths** we looked at probability. Just looking at the number of soldiers each side had before the Battle of Bannockburn, what was the probability of a Scottish victory? What was the ratio of English soldiers to Scottish soldiers? In **PE** we have looked at the difference between strategies and tactics in the case of William Wallace. Again, Bruce had a long term strategy and in each separate battle used very different tactics to achieve his long term strategic goal. In **English** we have looked at legends. How true do you think the legend of the spider actually is? Do you think this would be enough to inspire you to fight?

DID YOU KNOW?

Before Bruce's next battle at Bannockburn a small wooden box was shown to the Scottish soldiers. The box was covered in silver and bronze. Inside it were the bone relics of St Columba. This was said to have inspired Scottish soldiers before the battle. It is known as the Brecbennoch or the Monymusk Reliquary.

49

OUR EVERYDAY LIVES

Scotland's patron saint, St Andrew, probably never lived in Scotland. He was a fisherman and spread the Christian religion to modern day Turkey and Greece. The Romans crucified him in the 1st century AD. He was one of Christ's apostles and his brother, St Peter, became the first Pope. There is a legend that another saint was told to take Andrew's relics to Scotland. This he did, and he set up a church there in his name. St Andrew is also the patron saint of Russia. Russia has a saltire flag but the white and blue are reversed. St Andrew's day is celebrated in Scotland on 30 November each year.

VICTORY AT BANNOCKBURN

By 1314 Robert the Bruce had recaptured many castles from the English. Only one castle remained to be recaptured. Stirling Castle was in a key position in the centre of Scotland. The English soldiers in the castle needed supplies to survive and would need reinforcements. It was now more difficult for the English to get supplies to the castle as Bruce was regaining control of the country.

In 1307 Edward I died. He was replaced by his son Edward II. Unlike his father, Edward II was not a warrior king. Edward II preferred dancing, poetry and music to warfare.

Edward II's soldiers were marching towards the castle on the main road but had to take another route. Bruce's men had dug holes in the road and placed traps for the English cavalry.

Bruce was a strong war leader. He had planned and skilfully forced Edward II's army to take another route to the castle. Now the English were in a position with the Firth of Forth behind them. They were also surrounded by marshland. As nightfall came the English soldiers had to set up camp in this awful position. Bruce had the English army just where he wanted them. The night before the battle Bruce met with his commanders and gave a motivational speech. This inspired the Scots soldiers to do well in battle the following day.

Before the battle even started Bruce fought with an English knight called Sir Henry de Bohun. De Bohun was on horseback and charged at Bruce's horse. Bruce moved to one side to avoid being hit by the knight's lance. Then he hit de Bohun over the head with a battle axe. De Bohun was killed instantly. Bruce had shown he could lead from the front.

The following day Bruce's 6,000 men ran towards the English from woods at the top of a hill. The English had nowhere to retreat to. On one side was marshland and behind them was a river. Both would prove deadly for English soldiers who were already weighed down with heavy armour and weapons. Later in the battle Scots soldiers known as 'the Small Folk' joined the fighting. They only had farming tools as weapons. The English thought Bruce had another army and fled the battleground. This was a major victory for Robert the Bruce.

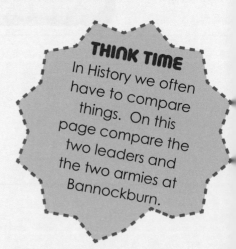

THINK TIME
In History we often have to compare things. On this page compare the two leaders and the two armies at Bannockburn.

PEOPLE AND EVENTS

Who had the most soldiers during the Battle of Bannockburn?

Compare the two Kings. Try to find at least two differences.

Which side do you think had the most chance of winning and why?

In a group make a list of reasons why you think Bruce won at Bannockburn.

With a partner decide which reason was the most important in the Scots victory.

Compare your answer with other partners in the class. Do you have the same answers? If not try to convince them that your answer is the right one.

Read the 'Did you know?' section on this page. Now write your own letter to the Pope. Convince him that Scotland should be free and Bruce should be king.

PEOPLE AND EVENTS IN THE MAKING OF SCOTLAND

MAKE THE LINK

In **Geography** maps can help us to understand why the Scots won the battle. In **English** we look at speeches. What sort of words inspire people? How are speeches delivered? In **Music** listen to Scottish music inspired by great Scottish victories. You may also want to compose music about Bannockburn.

Most of the Scottish army would have spoken **Gaelic** at Bannockburn. Do you know any Gaelic words? Lots of schools are teaching Gaelic as part of the curriculum.

DID YOU KNOW?

Far from being over in 1314, the Wars of Independence carried on until 1328. Berwick was not recaptured until 1318. In 1320 the Declaration of Arbroath was signed. It was a letter to Pope John XXII. It told him about all the things Edward had done to Scotland. It asked the Pope to help make Scotland free and to forgive Robert the Bruce for his past crimes.

51

OUR EVERYDAY LIVES

For years historians thought they knew the site where the Battle of Bannockburn was fought. However recently archaeologists have found clues under the ground which may mean the battle was fought in a different location. The first weapon to be found from the battle was discovered in 2004. It was an armour piercing arrow. History can change.

'IT CAM WI' A LASS'

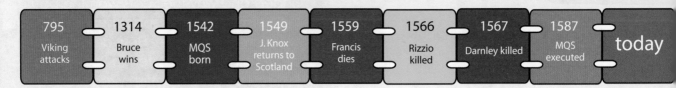

795	1314	1542	1549	1559	1566	1567	1587	
Viking attacks	Bruce wins	MQS born	J. Knox returns to Scotland	Francis dies	Rizzio killed	Darnley killed	MQS executed	today

1542 was a dangerous time to inherit the throne of Scotland. For a child it was even more dangerous. Relations between Scotland and England were like in Wallace and Bruce's time.

Henry VIII of England had been fighting a war against France. Scotland had strong links with France since Balliol had escaped and settled there. This was called the 'Auld Alliance'. Scotland's king, James IV, helped the French by attacking England. He hoped this would make Scotland look important. But at the Battle of Flodden in 1513, Scotland suffered a serious defeat. Tens of thousands of Scots were killed, including King James IV. This was a national disaster.

James V was heir to the throne but he was only seventeen months old. As he grew up, Scotland was under serious threat. It was a Catholic country and was under pressure from the Protestant, English king, Henry VIII. Both James' sons died in 1541. In 1542 the English attacked Scotland. The Scots were later defeated at Solway Moss. James V fell into a serious depression. He feared for Scotland's future. He said of the Scottish crown, 'It cam wi' a lass and it'll gang wi' a lass'.

On 14 December 1542, six days after the birth of his new daughter Mary, James V died. Henry VIII saw his opportunity. He attempted to marry his son, Prince Edward, to the baby Queen Mary. The Scots refused so Henry began to use

violence. This period was called the **Rough Wooing**. Henry invaded Scotland twice. In 1544 and in 1547 Henry burned down Edinburgh and destroyed important abbeys at Melrose, Kelso and Jedburgh. English soldiers then beat a Scottish army at the battle of Pinkie. Scots nobles did not help the new queen. Some nobles were greedy and looked after their own interests.

Mary escaped the violence by fleeing to France in August 1548. Her mother, Mary of Guise, was in the French royal family. So, the French king provided Mary with a ship for herself and her friends to escape. Her friends were known as 'The Four Marys'. The ship with them on board went around English warships and made it safely to France. There Mary Queen of Scots would be brought up in grand luxury. She wore stunning clothing, ate good food and lived well. She learned French, sang, danced, made music and wrote poems. Mary became more and more French each day.

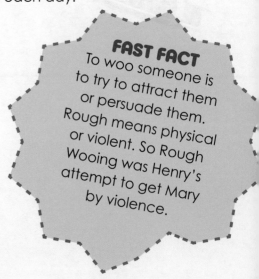

FAST FACT
To woo someone is to try to attract them or persuade them. Rough means physical or violent. So Rough Wooing was Henry's attempt to get Mary by violence.

52

ACTIVITIES

Make a list of problems facing Mary.

Explain why Mary enjoyed her time in France. Try to include three pieces of evidence in your answer.

When Mary was older she married the heir to the French throne, Francis II. A spectacular wedding took place at Notre Dame Cathedral in Paris in 1558.

Write a newspaper report telling readers about the wedding. It should contain the following things:

• Name of newspaper
• Date
• Appropriate short catchy headline
• Well written story
• Interviews
• Appropriate picture(s)

No expense would have been spared on the royal wedding. Clothing would have been bright, sparkly and magnificent. Design your own wedding clothes for the bride and groom.

MAKE THE LINK

This chapter will explore the friendships and conflicts between France, Scotland and England at this time. Nobles and royalty at this time would have spoken many different languages including French.

In **Art** we look at designs for clothing. Think how designs have changed over time. Some designs from history are used in modern clothing.

In **Geography** you might want to look at the route Mary took to escape from Scotland. She did not cross the English Channel directly. Instead she went from Dumbarton to Roscoff by going around Ireland. Why did she do this? Try to plot this journey on a map.

DID YOU KNOW?

53

Before her escape to France Mary hid in Inchmahome Island in Perthshire. Many years before, this had been a Celtic monastery. Buildings have their own history and have been used for lots of things and by different people through time.

OUR EVERYDAY LIVES

Mary Queen of Scots was born in Linlithgow Palace. Today, primary school students from the nearby primary school run an enterprising business in the palace. They organise guided tours of the palace and take the tours themselves. Not only do they conduct the tours but they do so in costumes that look like clothing from the time of Mary Queen of Scots. The costumes were made by the children. We have looked at the inspirational stories of Romulus and Bruce and the spider but this one must be the best! These students have a real 'can do' attitude!

TWO SUPERPOWERS RETURN

Mary Queen of Scots returned to Scotland in 1561 after her mother and her husband, Francis, both died. She was now a widow and very lonely. Scotland had changed a lot

since she left it as a young girl. When she left most Scottish people were **Catholic**. When she came back she found that many people had **protested** against the Catholic Church and formed a new religion. They called themselves **Protestants**. They even had their own prayer book. Important nobles were now joining this religion. They hoped that the new English Queen, Elizabeth I, would support them. Elizabeth was also a Protestant.

Mary arrived back on a wet, dreich day in August 1561. She hoped for a grand welcome from her subjects. However, many Scots now did not like Mary because of her religion. Some Scots disliked her even more when she tried to make her palaces more like the French ones.

A Protestant preacher, John Knox, met with Mary to tell her that she should marry a Protestant. He said this was the only way to keep the peace in Scotland.

John Knox returned to Scotland in 1555. His early life had been very eventful. He was born in Haddington and left to study at St Andrews University. Most jobs at this time were in the church.

Knox worked for the church but was not a priest. He was a lawyer. Then, he started to work with a man called George Wishart.

Wishart was trying to persuade Scots to join with Protestant England and abandon the Auld Alliance with Catholic France. David Beaton from the catholic Church was furious with this and had Wishart burned at the stake. This happened to many others who opposed the Church's rule, like Patrick Hamilton who was buried in 1528.

In an act of revenge, Protestants killed Beaton in St Andrews. Soon a large group of Protestants gathered in St Andrews. They listened to John Knox as he was a powerful speaker. Soon the meeting was broken up and Knox was arrested. He was sentenced to labour. This was hard work as he had to row the oars of a French galley ship as punishment. When he returned to Scotland he protested against the Catholic Church.

THINK TIME
Many people have been burned at the stake in Scottish history. Suspected witches were once burned. 'Heretics' who opposed the established church were also burned. Can you think of others who have died for their cause?

54

ACTIVITIES

BIASED REPORTING

GROUP 1

Write a short newspaper report on the return of Mary from a Protestant point of view. What sorts of feelings would be in this report?

GROUP 2

Write a newspaper report on the return of Mary from a Catholic point of view. What sorts of feelings would be in this report?

BOTH GROUPS

Remember the things you should have in a newspaper report:

• Name of newspaper
• Date
• Appropriate short catchy headline
• Well written story
• Interviews
• Appropriate picture(s)

ART CHALLENGE

Many pictures have been painted and drawn of Mary Queen of Scots since her return to Scotland. As in the above task, think about how Protestants and Catholics, felt about Mary's return of the Scottish queen.

Draw two pictures representing her return from two different points of view.

MAKE THE LINK

In **Religious, Moral and Philosophical Education** we learn about different religions and different ideas and ways of worship. You may want to find out more about how Catholic and Protestant churches are different from one another.

In **Modern Studies** and in **Personal and Social Education** we think about how conflicts can arise out of simple differences between groups of people. We also learn about how we can be more tolerant towards others and respect their differences.

DID YOU KNOW?

At the time of Mary Queen of Scots there were two major groups of people in the country, Catholics and Protestants. Since then people who worship other religions, or have no religion, have come to our country.
Today we live in a multicultural world.

55

OUR EVERYDAY LIVES

Across the world religion causes conflict between different groups of people. Recently in Iraq two different groups of Muslims (Sunni and Shia) have clashed with each other. In India there has been tension between the Hindu majority and the minority Muslim population. India was made independent from the British Empire in 1947. Part of the country was made into a Muslim country called Pakistan. Conflicts also arise in Palestine and Israel where Jewish Israelis clash with Muslim Arabs in the area. Scotland was no different at the time of Mary Queen of Scots because people were fighting over religion.

MARY AND MARRIAGES

Mary must have found life in Scotland very difficult. She seemed to be surrounded by enemies. She had to try to find a new husband so that there would be an heir to the throne. Many Scottish nobles wanted to marry her for power and money. Mary was suspicious of the nobles but knew that she had to try to keep them on her side. Many foreign princes also wanted to marry Mary.

She twice rejected offers from the heir to the Spanish throne. A foreign husband could cause even more problems for Mary and for Scotland. If possible she still wanted to find a Catholic husband living in Scotland. Mary soon found the perfect candidate. Henry Stewart (Lord Darnley) was royal, handsome and Catholic. They got married soon after they met.

However, Mary's happy relationship with Darnley did not last long. He was too vain and too silly to be with the queen of Scotland. He drank too much and was not a good companion for her. Soon Mary grew attached to her secretary. He was an Italian called David Rizzio. As well as working as her secretary he often played music for her and charmed her.

Darnley became jealous of Rizzio. Protestant lords were also concerned at how close Mary was becoming to Rizzio. They feared he was a Catholic agent. More bad news came for Protestants. Mary fell pregnant with Darnley's child. This would mean a Catholic heir to the throne. The lords tried to convince Darnley that Mary was having an affair with Rizzio. They told him that if Mary were to die

then he would become the king of Scotland This forced Darnley to act.

Mary was having supper with Rizzio early in the evening of Saturday, 9 March 1566. A group of Protestant lords broke into the queen's chamber in Holyrood House. They attacked the defenceless Rizzio. After a long scuffle Rizzio was killed. He was stabbed over 50 times. Lord Darnley's dagger was found in Rizzio.

While Darnley may not have killed Rizzio he was clearly involved. Darnley had even signed a proclamation against Catholics. This was read out to the Scottish people the following day. Mary fled to Dunbar Castle for safety. Here Mary gathered soldiers for a counter attack. Mary's soldiers managed to force many of the Protestant Lords out of the country. Mary once again held power in Scotland.

She began to regret marrying Darnley and turned now to the Earl of Bothwell. He owned Dunbar Castle. Bothwell was a tough man who appeared strong and ambitious. He would be a more stable husband. Mary preferred him to the childish Lord Darnley. In 1566 Mary gave birth to a boy. Now she had even less use for Darnley.

56

AND EFFECTS *

ACTIVITIES

1 Make a list of all the people that have appeared on the last page.

2 With a partner, discuss what each person has been doing so far in this section.

3 As a group explain why Mary needed a husband so quickly.

4 Describe what Mary hoped for in her new husband.

5 Explain why Rizzio was murdered by the Protestant lords.

6 What evidence is there that Darnley was involved in the murder?

7 With a partner, discuss if you have enough evidence to find Darnley guilty of the murder of Rizzio.

8 Compare the characteristics of Lord Darnley and the Earl of Bothwell. Remember that Darnley changed after he got married – include both descriptions.

Darnley	Bothwell

MAKE THE LINK

In **Personal and Social Education** you will discuss relationships and how they can change through time. In this unit we have seen how Mary felt about Darnley changing his behaviour. How do we react to this when it happens with one of our friends?

In **Modern Studies** you will look at how different countries are connected. Often they are connected by religion, this is something we might also look at in **Religious and Moral Education**.

DID YOU KNOW?

You can still see the room in which Rizzio was murdered. It is in Holyrood Palace in Edinburgh. The bloodstains used to be painted on so that one could still see where the murder happened. Rizzio was stabbed over fifty times in a cold-blooded killing. Mary had a pistol pointed towards her stomach so could do nothing.

57

OUR EVERYDAY LIVES

People can change their characteristics and behaviour for a whole range of reasons. Darnley appeared to be a good choice for Mary. However, shortly into her reign he changed his behaviour and she fell out of love with him.

EXIT DARNLEY ... ENTER BOTHWELL

Darnley became very ill. Because of his illness Mary had him live on his own away from Holyrood Palace. He stayed at a house called Kirk O' Field. On the night of 9–10 February 1567 Kirk O' Field was blown up in a huge explosion. Darnley was later found in the garden. He was wearing his night clothes and had a napkin stuffed in his mouth. His body did not appear to be burned.

WAS MARY RESPONSIBLE FOR KILLING DARNLEY?

Look at the evidence below:

- Mary fell in love with Bothwell.
- Mary disliked violence.
- Mary was catholic so could not divorce Darnley.
- Bothwell was seen laying a trail of gunpowder under Kirk O' Field.
- Soon after the murder, posters appeared in Edinburgh.
- Darnley's body was buried the same day he died.
- Mary did not go into mourning. She was spotted watching games soon after.
- Mary married Bothwell three months after Darnley's death.
- Bothwell was put on trial in April. He was found not guilty.

The Protestant lords were furious. They believed Mary had killed Darnley. They gathered an army and defeated Mary's army at a battle at Carberry Hill. Mary's new lover, Bothwell, escaped. He travelled to Orkney, Norway and then Denmark. There he was captured by the king of Denmark and died in a Danish prison. Mary was also captured and was sent to Loch Leven castle. Here she gave birth to Bothwell's children. Sadly, both children died at birth. Mary escaped but her army was again defeated. After defeat at Langside near Glasgow, Mary had only one person left to turn to. She went to England to ask for the support of her cousin – Elizabeth Queen of England.

ACTIVITIES

1 Place each piece of evidence listed opposite under the correct heading in the table below.

Mary was responsible	Mary was not responsible

2 Write a crime report for the incident at Kirk O' Fields.

Police report	
Date of incident	
Victim	Darnley
Possible witnesses	
Position of body	
Cause of death	
Impact of death on Scotland	

FAST FACT
The casket letters apparently showed Bothwell and Mary were having an affair. However, the originals were lost and the only copy was made by an Englishman.

MAKE THE LINK

In **Drama** we act out all sorts of scenes and show emotions. The murder of Darnley would be a good event to act out. The events surrounding the murder are very dramatic and the emotions after the event could be dramatised very well.

In **Science** we write reports. Think about how the style of report writing is different from the History report you are completing in activity 2.

In **Modern Studies** we are faced with decision making exercises. Like in activity 1, we have to decide what evidence can help us. Once we have done this we have to come to a final decision.

DID YOU KNOW?

The blue and white scottish saltire flag first made its appearance in Scottish history in AD 832. A Pict and Scots army were fighting the Northumbrians from England. Above the Lothian battlefield an X shaped cross appeared in the sky. It looked like the cross upon which St Andrew was crucified. The cross inspired the Scots to victory and has been used as the national flag since this event.

59

OUR EVERYDAY LIVES

Police use a variety of pieces of evidence from the scene of a murder. Their techniques are far more advanced than during Mary Queen of Scots' time. For example, police can now use fingerprints, DNA and also try to find CCTV footage of events. If these had been available at the time of Darnley's death we would be more certain as to who killed Mary's husband.

FAMILY MATTERS: ELIZABETH AND MARY

Elizabeth was not pleased to see Mary arrive in England. Elizabeth was a Protestant and Elizabeth's Scottish cousin Mary was a Catholic. Elizabeth was very scared of Mary because Elizabeth had no children. When she died there would be no Protestant heir to the throne of England. This worried Elizabeth. Some catholics thought Mary should be Queen of England. Elizabeth was Henry VIII's daughter. However, her mother, Anne Bdeyn was his second wife. Some people were not happy about this. The next person in line to the throne was Mary Queen of Scots, so Elizabeth put Mary in prison.

Mary was kept prisoner between 1568 and her eventual death in 1587. Elizabeth was a very worried woman. Some people living in England were Catholic and conspired to kill her. Many Catholics plotted to get Mary Queen of Scots onto Elizabeth's throne.

One plot was the Babington Plot. Anthony Babington was a Catholic noble. He sent Mary letters about a plan to **assassinate** Elizabeth. He also hoped that Spanish armies would invade England and free Mary. Letters about the plot were sent to and from Mary. They were sent in code so no one would find out. What they did not know was that Elizabeth had spies. They were reading the letters and breaking the codes. Babington was hanged for his part in the plot. Meanwhile, Mary was put on trial.

Mary was found guilty of being involved in plots to kill Elizabeth. She was sentenced to death but her cousin was very reluctant to sign the death warrant. Someone placed the death warrant in a large pile of letters that Elizabeth had to sign, she unwittingly signed the death warrant for Mary. At Fotheringhay, Mary was killed by having her head cut off. She was strong in her last moments. She spoke to her servants in French and told them not to cry. She then forgave the executioner and prayed. She wore a long black overcoat. Just before her final moment she removed it to unveil red clothing. It was her final act. The executioner axe fell three times before severing her head.

Both Elizabeth and Mary had protected their country from being taken over. Mary's son, James VI would inherit both countries. When Elizabeth died in 1603 she had no children. James became James the sixth of Scotland (VI) and James the first of England (I). James VI and I achieved what many had tried by fighting and war. He was king of Britain.

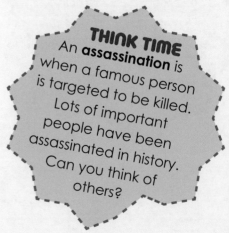

THINK TIME
An **assassination** is when a famous person is targeted to be killed. Lots of important people have been assassinated in history. Can you think of others?

60

ACTIVITIES

1 There have been lots of key people in this chapter. Earlier you made a list of people on one page. The chapter has lots more people in it. With a partner look through the chapter and make a list of everyone who has appeared in the chapter.

2 In a group, look at all the names on your list. Who do you think were the most important people in the life of Mary Queen of Scots? Put the names into a list in order of importance. The most important person should be at the top of the list and the least important person at the bottom of the list.

3 Using information in this chapter, make a timeline of the events in Mary Queen of Scots' life. Write out all the dates that have appeared in the chapter and next to the date a sentence about what happened on that date. If you have forgotten about timelines look back at page 8.

4 Come up with a code to send a message to someone else in the class. The message should read as follows (first, though, you must complete the blanks):

Mary spent _____ years in prison. She was executed in _____.

(Look at the 'Make the link' section to see some different types of codes and ciphers you could use.)

MAKE THE LINK

In **Maths** we look at codes and ciphers. These have been used throughout history to try to deceive people and to hide secret messages. There are lots of different codes and ciphers you could use. A simple one could substitute numbers or symbols for letters in the alphabet.

Another cipher used in Roman times was called the Caesar Shift. Caesar would agree a number with his generals. The number would be the number of times he would move letters up the alphabet. It would need to be kept a closely guarded secret. If the number was 3 the word HISTORY would appear as follows … KLVXRUB. Can you see how this has worked?

DID YOU KNOW?

Elizabeth I was perhaps one of the most powerful queens in British history. She led the country through a war against the mighty Spanish Armada. Recently films have been made about Mary and Elizabeth. These films are secondary sources. They are still useful to a certain extent.

61

OUR EVERYDAY LIVES

During the Second World War code breakers from Britain managed to break German codes. The Germans used a code which they thought was unbreakable. However, British mathematicians broke the code using the world's first computer. It was called the Colossus machine. They did not let people know they had broken the code so that they could still receive German messages. The information they received from the messages helped Britain to win the Second World War.

Today computers are a vital part of our lives.

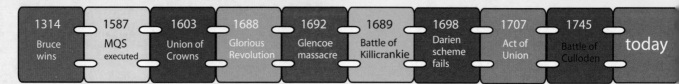

KINGS AND QUEENS

1314	1587	1603	1688	1692	1689	1698	1707	1745	
Bruce wins	MQS executed	Union of Crowns	Glorious Revolution	Glencoe massacre	Battle of Killicrankie	Darien scheme fails	Act of Union	Battle of Culloden	today

Understanding events in Scotland and Britain during the seventeenth and eighteenth centuries can be quite confusing. There are lots of people who were involved in turning points during this period. The parliaments of Scotland and England joined together and then there were lots of revolts against the kings and queens of Great Britain. These events happened for various reasons and each one was a **turning point** for the people involved. The kings and queens of Scotland were influential in these events. It is best to know the **chronology** of rulers.

PUT THE KINGS AND QUEENS INTO CHRONOLOGICAL ORDER:

James VII and II (1685–88)

Elizabeth of England (1558–1603)

Oliver Cromwell (1649–60)

Anne (1702–14)

William and Mary (1688–1702)

1. Mary Queen of Scots (1542–87)

Charles I (1625–49)

James VI and I (1603–25)

George I (1714–27)

Charles II (1660–85)

George III (1760–1820)

George II (1727–60)

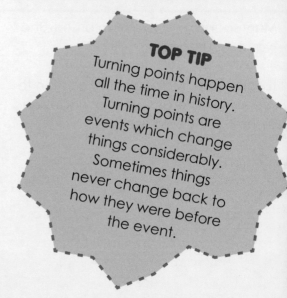

TOP TIP
Turning points happen all the time in history. Turning points are events which change things considerably. Sometimes things never change back to how they were before the event.

62

TURNING POINTS *

ACTIVITIES

1 Next to each monarch write out one fact about them. Use the internet to help you find information.

2 Look at the challenge on page twenty one of the *Active History workbook*. It asks you to make bookmarks for each of the key figures in the Scottish wars of Independence. You could do the same with the British kings and queens during this period.

OR

Look at the challenge on page thirty two of the *Active History workbook*. It asks you to make top trumps cards for different ships in Scottish history. You could do the same for kings and queens that you have come across in this unit. You could include 'year inherited throne', 'year left power', 'total years in power', 'male/female', 'age when died' and 'number of children' as headings.

MAKE THE LINK

In **Maths** you will look at the probability of events happening and the consequences of events happening. Looking at the Royal Family tree of Scotland and of Britain you could work out the probability of people falling heir to the throne. Sometimes it is not as easy as it looks as you will find out in this chapter.

In **Modern Studies** you will look at different arrangements for political decision making in different countries and at different levels in our country. Our country is a Constitutional Monarchy as you will see below. For a brief period there was no monarchy when Oliver Cromwell ruled as Lord Protector.

DID YOU KNOW?

The head of the British King or Queen appears on our stamps today. This has happened since 1840 when the first stamp, the Penny Black, was issued. The name of the country does not appear on our stamps because Britain was the first country in the world to issue stamps.

63

OUR EVERYDAY LIVES

Today we live in a Constitutional Monarchy. That means we have a Royal Family but also a government and a Prime Minister. Do you know who is in the Royal Family today? Do you know who is in the government and who the Prime Minister is?

REVOLUTION, REVOLTS AND JACOBITES

Under the kings and queens you looked at on the last page, Scotland took a series of important turning points. Many of these have shaped the way Scotland is today. An event known as the Glorious Revolution had a massive impact on Scotland and Great Britain.

The Glorious Revolution

English Members of Parliament were mostly Protestant and they did not like the Catholic King James VII and II. James thought he alone should rule but the Parliament wanted more power. Eventually, James was forced to leave. James went to France because it was a Catholic country. He was replaced with a Protestant called King William of Orange who ruled along with Mary, his wife, who was James' daughter. William came from the Netherlands.

English Protestants were delighted with the changes and called the event 'The Glorious Revolution'. Catholics did not support William and believed that James II's son should be the next king. He would have been James III. However the young James Francis Stewart did not inherit the throne. Some people called James Francis Stewart 'the Old Pretender'. The word pretender comes from a French word which means to claim. James Francis Stewart and a group called the Jacobites tried to rebel against King William.

The Jacobites wanted James Francis Stewart, to be on the throne. The word Jacobite comes from the Latin word for James – Jacobus. Many of the Jacobites came from the Highlands of Scotland.

However, William of Orange wanted to crush the Jacobites and any Highland clan chiefs who supported them.

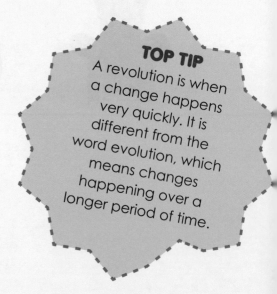

TOP TIP
A revolution is when a change happens very quickly. It is different from the word evolution, which means changes happening over a longer period of time.

TURNING POINTS *

ACTIVITIES

With a partner, discuss the reasons why James VII and II and the British Parliament had disagreements.

Look at the cartoon on the opposite page. It shows King James, William and Mary. Use your knowledge of events to add something into the speech bubbles and thought bubbles. What do you think they would be saying to each other? What do you think each person is thinking?

Where did James VII and II go to in 1688 and why do you think he went there?

Who was the next British king after James and why was the Parliament pleased about this?

What did the word 'Pretender' mean.

What does the word 'Jacobite' mean.

MAKE THE LINK

In **Religious, Moral and Philosophical Education** we might think about family structures. We may want to look at the Royal Family to see the various twists and turns that the British crown has taken as it has passed from monarch to monarch.

In **Modern Studies** we look at different ruling systems. Today we live in a Constitutional Monarchy whereby Britain is ruled by a king or queen and by the Parliament. The leader of the country is the Prime Minister. Think about who holds the most power in Britain today. Which other countries have a similar system?

DID YOU KNOW?

The English Parliament had two houses at this time, just as the British Parliament does today. Members of Parliament sit in the House of Commons while Lords sit in the House of Lords. These two houses make up Parliament. However, the Scottish Parliament only ever had one house.

65

OUR EVERYDAY LIVES

The Scottish Parliament is today situated at Holyrood in Edinburgh. It is just across the road from Holyrood Palace where David Rizzio was murdered. However, in the 1600s the Scottish Parliament was further up the High Street in Edinburgh. From 1639 Parliament was situated behind St Giles Cathedral.

MASSACRE AT GLENCOE

King William wanted to control the Highlands. He tried to bribe clan chiefs and crush the Jacobites who opposed him. King William forced Highland Clan Chiefs to swear allegiance to him. Sir John Dalrymple was given the job of making sure clan chiefs swore allegiance to the new king.

Many clan chiefs pledged allegiance to the king, like the Earl of Breadalbane. Some even sent men to join the kings army in their war with France. The deadline for swearing allegiance was 1 January 1692 but the MacDonalds Clan Chief MacIan arrived late. A snow storm delayed him getting to Inverary on time. Along the way he also arrived at the wrong place – Inverlochy! MacIan took the oath of allegiance on 5 January but he was too late. The list of names of those who had not sworn allegiance had already been written and sent. British soldiers were ordered to destroy the MacDonalds 'by fire and sword'. Opponents of King William would be shown no mercy.

English soldiers (called Redcoats) and some Campbells, who now supported William's army, arrived in Glencoe. The MacDonalds welcomed them as Highlanders do with most guests and visitors. The Campbells played cards with the MacDonalds before they all retired to their beds for the night. Early in the morning of 13 February, thirty-eight MacDonalds were murdered. It was a brutal killing because the victims were in their beds. Some MacDonalds tried to escape but they died of exposure in the snow.

TURNING POINTS *

ACTIVITIES

1 From your previous learning, explain who the Jacobites were.

2 Explain why MacIan did not swear allegiance on time.

3 Describe the Massacre of Glencoe.

MAKE THE LINK

In **Religious and Moral Education** we look at differences in religions and how these can lead to conflicts. We have made this link previously with Scottish history.

In **Geography** we look at extreme weather conditions and the effect the weather can have on people's lives. Weather partly led to the massacre at Glencoe and it also contributed to the fact that many of the MacDonalds who escaped did not survive.

DID YOU KNOW?

Sideburns became very popular at this time. Soldiers used muskets to shoot at the enemy. The musket had a small pan on the outside of the barrel for gunpowder. When the gunpowder exploded it fired the ball from the gun but could burn the next soldier along. To stop this, soldiers grew 'side burns' to protect their skin. Some believe the word originated from the American General Ambrose Burnside. He fought in the American Civil War between 1861 and 1865. Burnside was most famous for his facial growth than for success on the battlefield!

67

OUR EVERYDAY LIVES

Often we make promises, truces or agreements with friends, family and others. How often do we keep to our word? Do you think the government soldiers should have been more lenient with the MacDonalds? After all, they did eventually sign the agreement.

JACOBITES SCORE EARLY VICTORY

The Battle of Killiecrankie in 1689 could be said to be a turning point for the Jacobites and for Scottish history. They were fighting to put the exiled King James and his Stewart family back onto the British throne. Some said the battle was their high point. John Graham of Claverhouse would attempt to win back the throne for the Old Pretender, James Francis Stewart. Claverhouse had a fearsome reputation. He was also the Viscount of Dundee and more information on him can be found in the 'Did you Know' box. His enemies called him 'Bloody Claverhouse.' On the other hand his Jacobite followers called him 'Bonnie Dundee.'

In 1689 Jacobites had seized Blair Castle in Perthshire.This was despite the fact that the landlord there, the Marquis of Atholl, did not support the Jacobites. King William sent General Hugh Mackay into Scotland to deal with the Jacobites.Mackay made his way across Scotland.At a pass in the mountains near the river Garry Claverhouse had spotted Mackay's men on the move. The Jacobites hid in the mountains at a point known as the Passes of Killiecrankie. It was an area Claverhouse and the Jacobites knew well. There they watched the Redcoats march through in the most awful weather. Under foot conditions in the area were treacherous.

General Mackay and the Redcoats numbered over 4,000 men. There were only around 2,500 Jacobites hiding in the area. The main weapon for the Redcoats was the musket which had a long bayonet on the end of it. Some Jacobites had muskets but most used swords and a targe. Despite having more men Mackay was easily beaten by Claverhouse. The Redcoats fired artillery shots and their muskets. Neither of these worked and they quickly tried to fit their bayonets. Before they had time to do this, the Jacobites charged down hill with the feared Highland Charge. They cut down Redcoats with their swords as they charged. It was a great victory for the Jacobites. However, the Jacobites suffered a massive loss. Claverhouse was fatally wounded in the fighting. King William said that the Jacobite revolts were now over. Do you think Dundee's death would end the Jacobite revolts?

Despite William's comments the Jacobites did rise again. However, future attempted revolts also ended in failure. An attempt at rebellion in 1708 had failed when French soldiers sailing to Scotland were scared off by English warships. Further revolts in 1715 and 1719 also ended in failure.

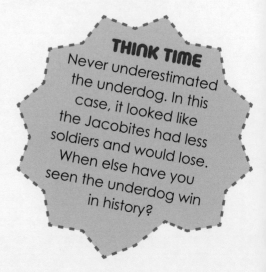

THINK TIME
Never underestimated the underdog. In this case, it looked like the Jacobites had less soldiers and would lose. When else have you seen the underdog win in history?

68

TURNING POINTS *

ACTIVITIES

1 Who led the Jacobites?

2 Who led the Redcoats?

3 Complete the following table using the information on the previous page:

	Advantages	Disadvantages
Jacobites		
Redcoats		

4 Write a newspaper report telling the readers about the two sides in the Battle of Killiecrankie and what happened. It should have the following things in it:

- Name of newspaper
- Date
- Appropriate short catchy headline
- Well written story
- Interviews
- Appropriate pictures.

5 Do you think that the Jacobites saw the Battle of Killiecrankie as a turning point?

6 Do you think that King William saw the Battle of Killiecrankie as a turning point?

MAKE THE LINK

In **Music** you might want to look at some of the music that was inspired by the Jacobites. Some of the songs can be quite rousing. Bonnie Dundee and Killiecrankie are just two examples of Jacobites songs your class may want to listen to. The words of the song also tell us much about history.

In **PE** look at long jump records and then look at the story below in the Everyday Lives section.

DID YOU KNOW?

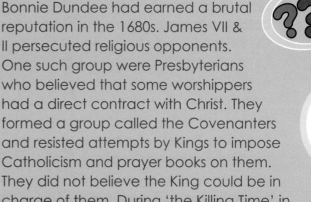

Bonnie Dundee had earned a brutal reputation in the 1680s. James VII & II persecuted religious opponents. One such group were Presbyterians who believed that some worshippers had a direct contract with Christ. They formed a group called the Covenanters and resisted attempts by Kings to impose Catholicism and prayer books on them. They did not believe the King could be in charge of them. During 'the Killing Time' in the 1680s Claverhouse acted for James VII & hunting out the Covenanters. King James VII & II saw them as a threat to his rule and wanted them removed.

69

OUR EVERYDAY LIVES

Today you can visit 'Soldier's Leap' at the River Garry in Perthshire. After the Battle of Killiecrankie many Redcoats drowned in the River Garry whilst trying to escape from the Jacobite Highland Charge. One solider was lucky. Donald Macbean managed to jump across the river. He jumped 18 feet right across the river. Do you think this is a legend or a true story?

DARIEN – A PLAN TO SAVE SCOTLAND

Scotland faced serious starvation after the massacre at Glencoe. Poor weather led to huge crop failures. In total 5% of the Scottish population died because of crop failures between 1692 and 1698. The Scottish Parliament became very concerned because Scotland was starving and very poor.

The Bank of Scotland was set up and plans were made to establish a Scottish **colony** overseas. William Paterson, from Dumfriesshire, had helped to set up the Bank of England and now planned to get enough money to send Scots overseas to a place called Darien in Panama. He promoted a new company called the Company of Scotland. Darien was between North and South America and was in a key position. It was close to America, the Caribbean and even the Far East. It would be easy to buy and sell things from here.

On 14 July 1698 fourteen ships left Leith, Edinburgh with 1200 men on board. Their mission was to build a Scottish colony at Darien, harvest successful crops and send food and money back to Scotland.

The plan ended in disaster. Very few of those who moved to Darien survived. The weather was much hotter than in Scotland and many Scottish settlers fell sick. Disease then spread quickly. During the worst days at least ten Scots died a day from malaria or yellow fever. To make matters worse, the Scots had not taken out enough supplies with them. Even worse still, Spain wanted to take over the colony. The Spanish managed to capture a Scottish ship. English ships nearby refused to help.

Discipline in the colony soon broke down as settlers resorted to chaos and drunkenness. Thousands of Scots had died and the Bank of Scotland was now broke. In total £400 000 was spent on the Darien Scheme and no profit was made. Some believe Scotland lost a quarter of its national wealth. Scotland was facing a major crisis.

Darien ●

FAST FACT
For a definition of the word **colony** look back at page 22.

TURNING POINTS *

ACTIVITIES

Explain why the Scots decided to set up a colony overseas.

Make a list of five reasons why the Darien Scheme failed.

Imagine you are working for William Paterson. You are asked to prepare a report for the Bank of Scotland asking for more money for a final expedition. Your report must include the following:

- An explanation of what the Darien Scheme plans to do.
- An explanation of the reasons why it failed.
- A list of suggestions to make the Darien Scheme a success.
- A summary of why the bank should give you money.

This needs to be **persuasive** and **convincing**.

Draw a poster advertising the Darien Scheme to Scots. Your poster should be bright and attractive but also contain lots of information.

MAKE THE LINK

In **Business Education** we look at where companies set up their businesses. Think about what sorts of things companies consider when situating offices and factories.

In both **Business Education** and **Maths** we might look at profit and loss. Accountants need to make sure that a company is making more money (profits) than losses. If it is not the company is insoluble and might become bankrupt.

In **Geography** and **Science** we look at the effect of weather and also at how different eco-systems work.

DID YOU KNOW?

Robert Burns is Scotland's favourite bard. His poetry and songs were often about key events in Scottish history. In 1791 he looked back at the events of this time. He believed Scotland was bought and sold for English gold, when it decided to join with England in 1707. He described those who signed the Act of Union as a 'parcel of rogues'.

71

OUR EVERYDAY LIVES

Piracy was a major problem for traders at this time. Despite the fact many people think pirates are from the past, piracy remains a problem today. Major trade routes are protected by the Royal Navy where possible. However, the pirates usually know the waters very well and are able to seize ships, goods and crew members. Often they demand very high ransoms to return ships and their crew.

DIVIDED NATIONS

Under the rule of the Kings and Queens you worked with earlier, there were a number of turning points for Scotland and for Britain. The Massacre of Glencoe was one of them. It changed relations between Scotland and England. It can be called a turning point because things changed.

In 1701 the tension between Scotland and England got even worse. A ship belonging to the Company of Scotland ran aground in China. It was called the Speedwell and had been trading there. Another Scottish ship called the Annandale was sent on a rescue mission. Before it got there it was captured and held by an English ship. The Scots retaliated. They captured an English ship and held it at Leith. They even hanged two of its crew for piracy! In England there were huge protests.

Relations got even worse when the Scottish Parliament and the English Parliament started to pass new laws.

The Scottish Parliament passed the Wine Law. It made sure that Scotland could buy and sell things without needing England to agree. The next law said that Scotland would not get involved in any of England's wars. Lastly the Scots passed a law saying that Scotland could pick its own King or Queen. It also said the Scots did not have to choose the same monarch as England. These laws infuriated many in England as Scotland could have its own trade, religion and King or Queen.

The English Parliament hit back. It passed a law called the Alien Law. It made it difficult for Scottish people to own a house in England or to trade things there. Many Scots needed to be able to sell sheep, cattle and

linen in England and so this was a serious problem.

Some Scots started to think it might be best to join with England. This might solve a lot of problems. A Union might stop a war between the two countries and would allow both countries to trade with each others. Also Scots would be able to trade with the huge worldwide Empire that England was building up. The English Parliament liked the idea of a Union because it would stop Scotland getting its own monarch.

In 1707 the Scottish and English Parliament joined in the Act of Union.However it was only agreed to after some fierce debates......

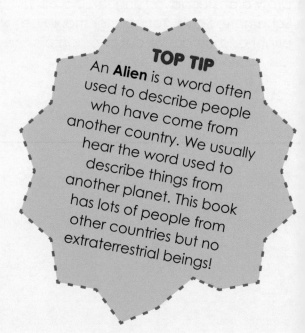

TOP TIP

An **Alien** is a word often used to describe people who have come from another country. We usually hear the word used to describe things from another planet. This book has lots of people from other countries but no extraterrestrial beings!

TURNING POINTS *

ACTIVITIES

1 Make a list of events which increased tension between Scotland and England.

2 Why do you think an English company might want to capture the *Annandale*.

3 Explain how the Alien Law in 1705 affected the Scottish people.

4 Which Law do you think caused the most tension? Give a reason for your answer.

5 Imagine you are part of the Company of Scotland. Write a letter to the English Parliament asking for the safe return of your ship, the *Annandale*.

MAKE THE LINK

In both **Personal and Social Education** and in **Religion and Moral Education** we learn about how to tolerate and cooperate with others. Toleration and cooperation broke down between Scotland and England again at this time. Try to think about reasons why good relations can break down.

In **Modern Studies** we look at conflict and cooperation. We also learn about the law. Think about how this has changed dramatically since the 1700s. When was the last time someone was hanged in this country?

In **Geography** we learn about mapping and we might want to look at which areas of the world the English East India Company was trading with. This may help to explain why it was so upset with a Scottish ship trading in China.

73

DID YOU KNOW?

Two days before the Act of Union came into effect a school of whales beached in Fife. The death of the thirty-one whales was taken by some as a bad omen.

OUR EVERYDAY LIVES

Every year Britain holds a series of events on the 5th of November. This is called Guy Fawkes Night. It was King James' decision to celebrate the night each year. Guy Fawkes and his fellow conspirators were caught before they could blow up the Houses of Parliament.

THE ACT OF UNION

There was a big debate in Scotland about whether to join with England or not. Some could not think of anything worse given the tension that existed between the two countries in recent years and in past history. Others thought there was a lot already uniting the two countries. Given Scotland's poor position there seemed no other solution to the ongoing problems.

The Union between Scotland and England was debated fiercely in coffee houses and public houses. It is still debated to this very day.

The English might tax us more

We want James to be our King, not a protestant

The Scottish Parliament have been bribed into joining with England

We speak the same language

If we unite there will be no wars between us

At least we can keep our own laws, church and education

If we unite we will get £400,000 compensation

TURNING POINTS ✱

ACTIVITIES

Why do you think so many members of the Scottish Parliament agreed to join with England? What do you think was the most important reason for them to sign the Act of Union?

For the Union	Against the Union

From what you have read, do you think joining with England would be a massive change for Scotland? Do you think it was a major turning point? Give a reason for your answers.

From 1707 onwards Scotland and England used the same money. Have a look at the coins in your pocket and see what sort of images appear on them. Make a list of the pictures on coins today and a list of pictures that might have been on coins in 1707.

MAKE THE LINK

In **Modern Studies** we look at decisions made by politicians and the reasons, or motives, they had for making these decisions.

In **English** we look at, write, hear and give speeches. There have been many famous speeches in history which have been very powerful. The Duke of Belhaven gave a very powerful speech against the Act of Union. Not only was his speech inspiring in terms of what it said, but it was delivered with a great deal of passion. In the workbook there is an activity relating to this speech.

DID YOU KNOW?

Squadrone Volante (see below) meant 'The Flying Squad'. They had twenty-five votes in the Scottish Parliament. Key members such as the Earl of Marchmont, The Duke of Roxburgh and the Marquises of Montrose and Tweeddale voted for the Union. Their votes were crucial in the Act of Union being agreed to in the Scottish Parliament.

75

OUR EVERYDAY LIVES

Various political parties were present in the Scottish Parliament at that time. Just like political parties today, each one had a different set of aims. The Court Party was for the Union as they supported Queen Anne and the British government. Key members included the Duke of Argyll and the Duke of Queensberry. The Country Party was opposed to the plans with the Duke of Belhaven delivering powerful speeches against the Union. Sitting in the middle was a party called Squadrone Volante.

JACOBITES SUFFER HEAVY DEFEAT

Not everyone was happy with the Act of Union. Some saw it as a negative turning point for Scotland. In Scotland Jacobites still opposed the King. They still wanted a Stewart descendant of James on the throne.

In 1745 another revolt offered a possible turning point for Jacobite fortunes. This revolt was led by the "Young Pretender". He was Charles Edward Stewart, the grandson of James VII & II. He was called Bonnie Prince Charlie and led what Jacobites affectionately called 'The '45 Rebellion'. He hoped to catch the English off guard as they were fighting a war against France. Charlie returned to Scotland from France. He captured Edinburgh and then defeated Redcoats at the Battle of Prestonpans. Charlie now attacked England. He marched through Lancaster, Preston, Manchester and Derby. He even got within 150 miles of London. However, Charlie failed to get the huge number of supporters he hoped for and had to march home. The new King, George II, brought troops back from abroad. The two armies met on Culloden Moor near Inverness. On the night of 15th April 1745 the Jacobites took part in a night raid on the Redcoats camp at Nairn. The raid was unsuccessful and left the Jacobites exhausted, hungry and sleep deprived the following day. Charlie was advised by his commanders not to fight. However Charlie lined his men up on a boggy, marshy battlefield at Culloden.The Jacobite forces were outnumbered and outwitted by the Government commander, the Duke of Cumberland.

Cumberland had 18 artillery canons and 9,000 men. Their first shots did not have much success but it was a sign of things to come. Charlie and his 6,000 men had no chance of winning. His secret weapon, the Highland Charge, could only be used as a surprise. It could not be used in open ground and not fighting uphill in such boggy conditions. When the Jacobites charged the Redcoats knew what to do. Cumberland had trained his men to wait until the Jacobites lifted their swords before stabbing them with their bayonets. Each Redcoat attacked the Jacobite to his right so that the bayonet could not be brushed away by the Jacobites targe. This new skill worked. Cumberland only suffered a few hundred casualties. Meanwhile Jacobite casualties were well over one thousand. After the battle Cumberland ordered his Redcoats to kill any injured Highlanders on the battlefield. Cumberland then started to destroy Highland culture.He attacked many Highland homes and killed many innocent women and children.Cumberland also banned Highlanders from playing bagpipes and wearing tartan plaid.Then he banned them from speaking Gaelic. Clan Chiefs lost their land and had their houses burned down. Later they were replaced by new landowners. The Clan chiefs were father like figures to Highland families. Highland culture was changing. It was a major turning point .

ACTIVITIES

With a partner make a list of reasons why the Jacobites were defeated at Culloden.

With a different partner make a list of things Cumberland did to try to destroy Highland culture after the battle.

Do you think that the Battle of Culloden was a turning point for the Jacobites? Give a reason for your answer then compare your answer with others in your group.

Do you think that the Battle of Culloden was a turning point for the Highlands? Give a reason for your answer then compare your answer with others in your group.
Read the Did You Know box.

Produce a wanted poster for Bonnie Prince Charlie.

TOP TIP
Culloden Moor was called Drummossie Moor at the time of the battle

MAKE THE LINK

In **Geography** you could find a map and trace Bonnie Prince Charlie's route. Use the scale to try to work out how far he travelled. Look not only at the distance travelled but the terrain of the land. In **Modern Studies** you look at culture and how people behave in a society. We also look at people's rights, like those of the Highlanders. We also look at reasons why a group might not be treated equally and how we can solve these problems.

In **Religious, Moral and Philosophical Education** we look at issues of morality. We might want to think about the morality of Cumberland's actions. Many children in Scotland learn **Gaelic** as part of their education. You have seen in this chapter how Cumberland tried to destroy this part of Highland culture.

77

DID YOU KNOW?

After Culloden Bonnie Prince Charlie was a wanted man. A reward of £30,000 was put up for his capture. He moved from place to place and hid in the Highlands and Islands. In 1746 he was smuggled to Skye by Flora MacDonald disguised as her servant, Betty Burke. He eventually escaped to France. Flora MacDonald was not so lucky! She was captured and taken to the Tower of London for her crime. She was later freed. Charlie never returned and died in Rome as a drunk!

OUR EVERYDAY LIVES

Then, and today, culture was important in people's lives. Culture is when people share the same ideas, likes, tastes and ways of living. Importantly they are able to share and express them. Think about the things that are important to our culture - is it language, music or dress? What would upset you the most if it was removed?

LIFE IN THE HIGHLANDS

1745 AD	1792 AD	1816 AD	1846 AD	1965 AD	1969 AD	today
Battle of Culloden	Cheviot introduced	Trial of Patrick Sellar	Potato famine	Money into Highlands	Oil found in North Sea	

Life in the Highlands before and after Culloden was a pretty bleak and harsh existence. Conditions were poor compared to today and the work was hard. Highlanders worked mainly on farms. Here they would work for a landlord but also keep animals and some crops to feed themselves. They worked long hours, from sunrise until dusk. Most of the work was done by hand. Tools were very basic and machines had not yet been invented.

Living conditions were not much better. Highlanders lived in stone houses that were built for both humans and animals to live in. The roofs were made from timber beams, turf, heather and some straw. The walls were a ramshackle of stones. There was no mortar to hold the stones together. The floor was also stone although some had wooden floors. Either way it was cold and dirty. Some houses had spaces for windows which allowed in fresh air; however, there was no glass double glazing like today. Fresh air was a good thing in the summer but in the winter it would be extremely cold. Houses without windows would be very dark. The only light came from candles made from animal fat and old cloth or wool. Each house had a large fire for light, cooking and heating. Most Highlanders burned peat on this fire. There was only a small vent for smoke to leave the house. This could be very smoky and smelly as the houses did not have a chimney. Added to this smell was the smell of animals. Small animals like chickens and pigs would walk in and out of the house and some houses had a byre next to the living area to keep cattle. In most houses everyone lived in one room.

People had their own beds. These were wooden box beds which had straw as padding. You would have to sleep with your mouth closed, though. As well as rain water coming from the roof, worms and bugs would often fall from the turf and heather!

Most Highland houses had basic kitchenware such as bowls, pots and cutlery but only a few items to decorate the house. There might have been a table, chairs and a cupboard for keeping personal items in.

In the summer some Highlanders would move to small stone houses in the higher ground called shielings. They would want to take their cattle to higher ground for pasture

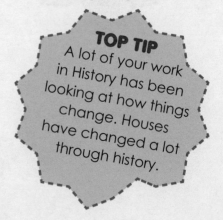

TOP TIP
A lot of your work in History has been looking at how things change. Houses have changed a lot through history.

78

INTERPRETING EVIDENCE

ACTIVITIES

With a partner, make a list of all the things you would **not** like about living in the Highlands at this time.

In your group compare a Highlander's house to the houses we found out about earlier at Skara Brae. Explain which parts of the Highlander's house you think are better. Are there any parts which are the same? Is there anything that is worse about the Highlander's house?

Following your discussions, try to complete the following table.

Features of house	Skara Brae	Highland house	My house
Number of rooms			
Protection from the weather			
Living area			
Where to cook			
Where to sleep			
Where to store food			
Where to store personal items			
Walls			
Roof			
Security			

Using the food in the Home Economics 'Make the link' section, devise a menu for a three course evening meal.

MAKE THE LINK

In **Art** we could think about how Highlanders decorated things. Plants were often used as dyes to add some colour to clothing and other items.

In **Craft and Design** we look at designs and shapes for houses and shelters.

In **Home Economics** we think about food supplies and making meals. Most Highlanders had oatmeal which they mixed with milk or water to make porridge. They used animals, such as chickens, sheep and cattle, for meat. Some Highlanders would cut into cattle's veins to drain animal blood which they could mix in with the oatmeal. Some had eggs, and even fish if they were close enough to the coast. Cheese could be made although it took some time.

DID YOU KNOW?

79

A **But 'n' Ben** was the name given to a small Highland cottage that had two rooms. In the Highlands there are many of these which you can still see today.

OUR EVERYDAY LIVES

The government had no responsibility for housing in the 1700s and 1800s. However, in the twentieth century the government became more and more involved in people's lives. They have passed laws to ensure bad quality housing is knocked down. The government also built council houses. They have also built new houses. Today, most new housing is built by private companies. Look at the different types of housing in your area.

CHANGES IN FARMING

Farming changed greatly in the Highlands in the late 1700s and early 1800s because of **new technology** and **new methods of working.**

Up to the 1800s most people who lived in Scotland worked in **agriculture (farming).** Most worked on small farms making enough food to feed their family and some extra to sell. They did not produce much food and did not make much money.

Tools had only changed a bit since Skara Brae stone tools and Celtic iron tools. Farmers would still use hand tools. The land was split up using the **run rig system.** Earth was made into little mounds and seeds were hand planted on top of these mounds. This was so that rain water would run into the space between the mounds and not ruin the crop seeds. It took a long time to plant and did not make many crops. Sometimes animals would come into the run rigs and eat any crops that had grown. Fences were not used to keep them out.

Changes in farming were to have a major impact on Highlanders' lives.

Changes in farming
1. **New technology** – machines were invented for planting and gathering crops. At first they were pulled by animals like oxen or horses but later they were steam powered.
2. **Drains** were put under the soil to stop rain water from ruining crops. Rubble and sand helps rain water drain away.
3. Because new machines needed flat land to run over and drains were being better used there was now no need for runrigs. More crops are produced each harvest time.
4. Fences were put around the land to keep animals out and for stock control.

Some farmers may have liked the changes as new technology meant the work was easier, but it also caused huge problems for Highlanders. After 1815 the new machines could do the work of ten men so many farm workers lost their jobs. They left the Highlands to look for work elsewhere.

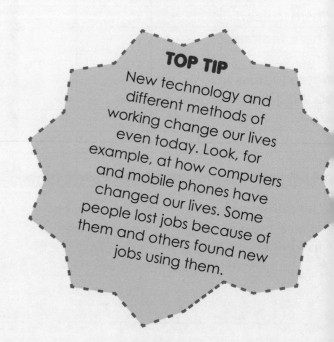

TOP TIP
New technology and different methods of working change our lives even today. Look, for example, at how computers and mobile phones have changed our lives. Some people lost jobs because of them and others found new jobs using them.

80

ACTIVITIES

1 Which change do you think was the most important for Highlands.

2 In your groups discuss whether new technology has been a good thing or a bad thing for Highlanders. Think about the new technology that you use in your life and the benefits and drawbacks it has on our lives.

3 Complete the following table.

Advantage of new technology	Disadvantage of new technology

MAKE THE LINK

In **Craft, Design and Technology** we look at how machines and technology have changed. We also learn about how they have affected the way people work and live.

In **Geography** we look at changes to farming and land use.

In **Biology** you may look at crop rotation and how farmers put different crops on the land at different times so that all the nutrients are not taken out the soil and the land can be used in future years.

In **English** you may want to look at Robert Burns's poems. Many are about life on a farm.

DID YOU KNOW?

Barbed wire was first used on American farms but it was soon used to protect soldiers from the enemy in the First World War. Today, barbed wire is still used on some farms and is also used to help keep intruders out of important buildings.

81

OUR EVERYDAY LIVES

Farming is still an essential part of British life. Farming produces much of what we eat every day. Anything we cannot make on our own farms, we need to buy from other countries. This is called importing. It is expensive to do this. On the other hand, we can also sell what we make on our farms. Selling to other countries is called exporting. Can you see how the materials coming **in** are called **imports**. They both start with an 'i'. Materials **exiting** our country are called **exports**. Both start with an **'e'**.

PUSH AND PULL FACTORS

Some say that people left the Highlands long before the new technology came in. Some say it all started with the failed Jacobite revolts led by Bonnie Prince Charlie. After this the British government imposed laws which tried to bring an end to Highland culture. We learned about these in the previous chapter.

People did not leave the Highlands overnight. It happened over a long period of time. Many Highlanders had a big decision to make at this time.

Some Highlanders were attracted abroad to places like America, Australia and Canada. Some even moved to other places within Scotland, especially in the big cities of Glasgow, Edinburgh and Dundee. Other decided to stay in the Highlands.

Should I stay in the Highlands or should I go somewhere else?

Should I stay or Should I go?

- I could meet a girl in the city and get married.
- The government destroyed Highland life after Culloden.
- I only speak Gaelic. In the cities they speak English.
- Glasgow and Edinburgh have factories and well paid jobs.
- Sheep farms have taken over our land and do not need workers.
- My grandmother still lives with us and cannot move.
- Factory work is indoors and warm.
- My family have lived here for generations.
- My land has been sold for deer hunting.
- I only know farming, I have no other skills. The potato famine in the 1840s has left my family starving.
- People can buy cheap boat tickets to Canada.
- I have seen posters showing sunny Australia and America where there is lots of land.

INTERPRETING EVIDENCE

ACTIVITIES

1 Which three Scottish cities was the Highlander on the opposite page thinking of moving to?

2 Which three countries was the Highlander thinking of moving to?

3 Complete the following table using the information on the other page.

Reasons to stay	Reasons to go

4 Make a list of reasons that are pushing him out of the Highlands.

5 Make a list of reasons pulling him to move somewhere else.

MAKE THE LINK

In **Music** we hear all sorts of songs. Music, songs and instruments travel with people. Listen to music from some other countries and also try to find out where Scottish music is still played in the world today.

In **Geography** you will look at population movement and the reasons why people move from one country to another. You will look at push and pull factors here as well.

In **Business Education** you will look at advertising. You might want to consider what sort of adverts and posters the Scottish Patriotic Society made that convinced Highlanders to move to places like Australia and America.

There are lots of books and poems written about the Highland Clearances – ask your **English** teacher to read some of them with you.

There are some famous paintings of the Clearances which you might want to look at in **Art**. For example, Thomas Faed's painting 'Last of the Clan'.

83

DID YOU KNOW?

Scotland comes second in terms of the number of its people to emigrate. It is second alongside Norway. Ireland is the leading country for people emigrating.

OUR EVERYDAY LIVES

Today Scotland has many immigrants from a number of different countries. Some of them have been **pushed** out of their own countries. Others found Scotland an attractive country to live in and were **pulled** towards Scotland.

WERE LANDLORDS SCAPEGOATS?

The Highland Clearances is the name given to the long period of time when a large number of people left the Highlands of Scotland. Historians still debate about the landlords' role in the Highland Clearances. Some criticise the landlords for violently throwing innocent Highlanders off their land. They did not help the poor and starving. Other historians defend the landlords. They say the Highlands needed to be changed. Highlanders were not making enough money to make profits or even to survive and had to move.

Some Highlanders left the area before they were thrown off the land. Others were evicted from (thrown out of) their homes by the landlords. We need to decide whether the landlords were greedy and evil people who should be criticised or whether it was best that the Highlanders leave as things had changed.

TOP TIP

A **scapegoat** is someone who gets the blame for something that is not their fault. In this section you can decide if the landlords were in fact scapegoats.

Increasing numbers of people lived in the Highlands **but** there was not enough land or food for them.

Clan chiefs and Bonnie Prince Charlie failed to beat the British government in the 1745 and the 1746 revolts. Clan chiefs' land was given to new landlords. The clan chiefs cared for Highlanders like family members. The new landlords only wanted to make money.

The landlords did not think Highlanders made enough money from farming so they threw them off the land to make way for sheep farming and deer hunting estates.

Prices of wool, cattle and kelp were falling and Highlanders were not making enough money to survive so they had to leave.

The Highlanders had tried to set up factories in Inverury and Loch Fyne but these all failed.

Almost three quarters of a Highlander's diet consisted of potatoes. A fungal disease called blight killed the potato crop in 1846. Mass starvation followed.

INTERPRETING EVIDENCE

ACTIVITIES

1 Complete the following table using information from the opposite page.

Landlords to blame for Clearances	Other factors to blame

2 In groups, discuss who was to blame for the Highland Clearances. Get someone in your group to write down what everyone thinks.

Look back at what you have all said after you have completed the next page. Have your opinions changed?

MAKE THE LINK

In **Modern Studies** and **Geography** you might look at natural disasters and the impact on the people who live in the countries where these have happened. What causes natural disasters and what are the consequences of them? Think about what we can do to help when a natural disaster happens.

In **Business Education** we think about profit and loss. A profit is when someone makes money. A loss is when someone spends more money than they have coming in.

DID YOU KNOW?

In 1845 the potato crop in Ireland failed causing mass starvation. In 1846 Scotland was hit with the same problem. The potato famine was much worse in Ireland and caused thousands to die. Many Irish emigrated to Scotland. They found work in the big cities like Glasgow, Edinburgh and Dundee. They also set up new football teams like Celtic, Hibernian and Dundee Hibernian (after 1909 called Dundee United).

85

OUR EVERYDAY LIVES

Even today starvation can cause great suffering and can cause some people to have to move quickly from one area to another to survive. Sometimes the British government sends food or help to areas suffering from starvation.

TRIAL OF PATRICK SELLAR

Patrick Sellar was a factor. A factor's job is to look after the land for the landlord. Sellar was given the job of evicting some Highlanders living on the Duke of Sutherland's land. Sellar is often seen as a scapegoat for the Highland Clearances. In this section you need to interpret evidence to decide if he is guilty or innocent.

Sellar's trial took place at Inverness High Court in 1816. Those accusing Sellar of crimes spoke in Gaelic and their testimony had to be translated into English for the jury. The jury was made up of landlords, a lawyer and a rich merchant. The two main witnesses were William Chisholm and Henrietta Mackay. Chisholm's mother-in-law, Margaret Mackay, died after a fire in their house and Sellar was accused of causing her death.

> Sellar ordered my house to be set on fire. The old woman was 100 years old. She could not get out. Her blankets caught fire and she died five days later.

> You are accused of killing a woman by arson. This is wilful fire raising. And you demolished a mill. Your sheep have also eaten the people's corn. You are of good character. How do you plead?

> Not guilty! These things did not happen because I was cruel. If the sheep ate people's corn is because my sheperds were careless, the people should have told me. I would have done something about it

86

At the end of the case the judge told the jury that they had heard lots of evidence from both sides. He said that this can be confusing. He said if the jury were confused that they should think about the good character of Sellar. The jury were also told that Sellar was only following the orders of the landlord, the Duke of Sutherland.

The case lasted all day and into the night, it only took the jury thirty minutes to come to a decision. The jury acquitted Sellar.

TOP TIP
In Scots law there are three decisions a court can take. Not guilty, guilty or not proven. The last means that the judge thinks they might be guilty but there is not enough evidence to prove it.

INTERPRETING EVIDENCE

ACTIVITIES

1 Re-enact the court case in your classroom:

STEP 1: Choose a judge from your class. Who would be fair, and able to hear both sides of the case?

STEP 2: Choose a jury – they should be good listeners. They should also be good at decision making.

STEP 3: Make two teams – prosecution and defence. They must be good at debating.

STEP 4: Each team should produce a speech. Decide who is going to deliver the speech or if it will be a team effort.

STEP 5: Let the judge and jury decide.

2 Historians need to be very careful of bias. Sometimes people have a reason not to tell the whole truth or only to give their opinions.

a) Read the above information in the Did you know box. Do you think it is factually accurate or biased? Discuss with a partner.

b) Is MacLeod's report useful given how long after the event it was written? Give a reason for your answer.

c) Why do you think Donald MacLeod might be biased or one sided?

MAKE THE LINK

In **English** you will need to use evidence to help make a case when you are writing. Ask your English teacher if you can set up a mock court trial with judges, jury, witnesses, and defence and prosecution lawyers. Prepare speeches for each part to convince the jury. In **English** you also need to be careful when you are reading information just in case it is biased and only giving you one side of the story!

In **Modern Studies** you will take part in lots of decision making exercises just like the one we have just completed. You will need to read lots of information and then use it to come to a final decision.

DID YOU KNOW?

87

Donald MacLeod lived in the Highlands during the Clearances. In 1857 he wrote letters to a newspaper in Edinburgh which provide us with useful information on the eviction of people in the Highlands. MacLeod accused Sellar of shouting, 'Damn her, the old witch, she has lived too long, let her burn' during the eviction of the Mackays.

OUR EVERYDAY LIVES

Every day we read, see and hear stories and reports in the newspapers and on the TV and radio. We listen and speak to people all the time. Being able to detect bias is an important skill. We need to be aware when people are giving us unfair opinions. This can mean what they are saying has been exaggerated or is not true.

THE HIGHLANDS TODAY

The Highlands **changed** dramatically from a land filled with farmers to a land with lots of sheep and deer. Sheep farming made more profits for the landowners. Deer hunting was also a good way to make money. The Highlands were almost deserted. However, in recent times the Highlands have became an attractive place to live.

In 1965 the British government put money back into the Highlands. The government also set up the Highlands and Islands Development Board to help the area and provided some much needed money.

Highlanders had struggled to be successful with fishing around the time of the Highland Clearances as they did not have the money to buy the necessary equipment to get started. However, today fishing is a major employer in the north of Scotland. You will find out some more about this in the next chapter.

Also, many in the area now work in the North Sea oil industry. Oil was discovered under the North Sea in 1971. Since then lots of money has been made from it. There are lots of jobs working with the oil and gas that can be found beneath the North Sea. Many people work on oil rigs like the one seen in the picture.

Probably the most important thing in reviving the Highlands has been tourism. Many tourists now visit the Highlands to look at the spectacular landscape and to discover more about scotland's history and take part in adventure holidays. Ski resorts, 4x4 off-road driving, hunting and water sports all attract tourists.

As was mentioned earlier in the book, some people like the idea of having an old historic house. Many people who live in the cities have bought old black houses and renovated them as holiday homes for the summer holidays. The Highlands of Scotland are once again an attractive place to live in and visit.

CTIVITIES

Make a list of jobs that people might do in the Highlands and Islands today.

Give four reasons why tourists from overseas might want to visit the Highlands.

You have been employed by a new hotel in the Highlands. You have been asked to make a poster and a leaflet to attract foreign tourists to the hotel and to the Highlands. Think about what sort of things attract people to the Highlands. Also think about what sort of things would make tourists want to use your hotel. Use all these 'selling points' in the poster.

The hotel wants to attract a wide range of tourists to the hotel and wants them to come from across the world. Translate your poster and leaflet into two foreign languages.

MAKE THE LINK

Completing the poster task in French, Spanish or German will require your **Modern Languages** skills. What other languages do you know or are spoken by your classmates? You could have a number of different posters in many different languages.

Posters and adverts need to be well presented to help make the Highlands look attractive to visit. **Computing Studies** may be able to help you use computer packages to make the posters look professional.

In **Art** you could think about the sorts of pictures you might want to include in the poster. Then think about how you would design the poster and lay out the text, images and any information for tourists.

89

DID YOU KNOW?

The oil that was found under the North Sea is worth millions of pounds. The oil fields in the North Sea are named after sea birds. 'Auk' oil field was discovered in February 1971. Since then Brent, Cormorant, Dunlin, Eider, Fulmar and Gannet have opened. However, the oil fields will not last forever and we need to look for alternative sources of energy.

OUR EVERYDAY LIVES

Tourism is one of Scotland's leading employers today and brings in a lot of money to Scotland. Look in your local area to see where tourists stay, what they go to see and where they spend money. What sorts of jobs are available in the tourist industry?

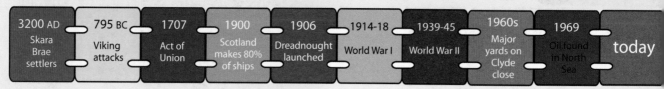

SCOTLAND AND THE SEA

| 3200 AD Skara Brae settlers | 795 BC Viking attacks | 1707 Act of Union | 1900 Scotland makes 80% of ships | 1906 Dreadnought launched | 1914-18 World War I | 1939-45 World War II | 1960s Major yards on Clyde close | 1969 Oil found in North Sea | today |

Britain is an island. It is surrounded by water and so the sea is very important to Scotland. It is from the sea that we have been invaded, as we have seen in chapters 1 and 2. The sea has also brought us lots of useful things. We have been able to send our goods to other countries (this is called **exporting**) where we have sold them for money. We also buy goods from other countries (which is called **importing**). Anything to do with money or buying and selling things is called an **economic** factor. The sea has become very important to Scotland's economy.

Ships were not just important to Scotland to trade things. Ships allowed Scots to travel, like in chapter 6 when many Scots left to go to Australia, America, Canada and other countries.

Fishing has also been important to Scotland since settlers lived at Skara Brae. Fishing boomed in Scotland, at the start of the 1900s. Well over two million herrings were cured in Scotland. After being cured at ports like Mallaig on the west coast, fish was often exported to places as far away as Germany and Russia. The boom in fishing was interrupted in the 1900s by two world wars.

During a war the sea was still important. We had to build ships to defend our country. The navy is like the army, as it defends our country from attack. It is made up not of soldiers but of sailors who fight on battleships. The navy is another way in which the sea is very important for Scotland.

A summary of Scotland's connections with the sea:

Trade: exporting and importing goods to and from other countries.

Travel: emigration and immigration: many Scots left to go overseas. Likewise, other people have come to Scotland by sea.

Defence and war: the navy defends our shores against foreign invasion.

Food and jobs: fishing is still a huge employer in Scotland's coastal towns.

TOP TIP

Trade can happen in many ways. School students sometimes trade charms, football cards or computer games. Scottish traders have become very wealthy. They buy things and then sell them to someone else for a higher price. This is trading.

90

CAUSES AND IMPACT *

ACTIVITIES

From a previous chapter give an example of Scottish people being attacked from the sea.

From a previous chapter give an example of Scottish people using the sea to travel far away.

Define the word **export**.

Define the word **import**.

Think of three items we need to export to Scotland because we cannot find or make them here **and** think of three items Scotland makes and sell overseas.

Put your items into the table below:

Scotland's imports	Scotland's exports

MAKE THE LINK

In **Maths** we may think about how an item can become more expensive from when is made in one country to when it is sold somewhere else in the world. Think about how does the price of an item go up.

In **Physics** we investigate displacement and how ships float.

In **Business Education** you may look at the sorts of items Scotland imports and exports today. Think about what Scotland might export in the future. This is what will make profit in the future!

In **Geography** you could look at the areas of Scotland where ships are made? Why was the Clyde so popular with shipbuilders?

DID YOU KNOW?

People who use the sea are protected by the Royal National Lifeboat Institute. The RNLI was founded in 1824. It was founded by Sir William Hillary who lived on the Isle of Man. From his home he saw lots of ship wrecks. Today the RNLI has over 40 000 volunteers who work aboard lifeboats, lifeguard our beaches, work at lifeboat stations and help fundraise. Over 130 000 lives have been saved by the RNLI since it was set up.

OUR EVERYDAY LIVES

Scotland still has a great connection with the sea. Coastal towns like Eyemouth, Kinlochbervie and Anstruther have strong connections to the fishing industry. Other jobs at sea include the Merchant Navy and lots of jobs trading across the world. Recently many people have found work in the North Sea on oil rigs. How many of you will work in jobs which are connected to the sea?

SCOTLAND'S SHIPBUILDING BOOM

Scotland once built a lot of ships. The shipbuilding industry was most successful in the early twentieth century. When factories or industry have a successful time this is called a 'boom'. In 1900 Britain was producing 80% of the world's ships so it certainly was a boom. But what were all these new ships being built for?

New ships were needed for various reasons. In the nineteenth century many wooden ships were built in areas like Aberdeen and Dundee. However wooden sailing ships were soon to be replaced with steel ships that were steam powered. The Steam Revolution was led by a Scotsman, James Watt. He perfected the steam engine. This led to major changes in transport. Later, Scottish engineers like David Napier pioneered steam navigation and then steel ships. These ships were desperately needed to move imports and exports around the British Empire. Scotland was part of Britain at this time. Some said that Glasgow was the second city of the Empire. Glasgow built many ships for the Empire. In 1812 the comet became the first steam ship to sail down the Clyde. From then the boom quickly took off as the graph shows.

The *Comet* ran passengers from Greenock to Glasgow it was Europe's first commercial steamboat service. After the *Comet*, further improvements were made to create to ships capable of longer journeys. The *Comet* was a wooden vessel. But soon all ships were made from steel.

THINK TIME
Shipyards would need to be close to where they could find materials for making ships. Think about where factories are built today and how they get materials to them.

Most of the new ships were built on the River Clyde. The area around the Clyde had all the materials that were needed to build and power the ships. Coal and iron were easily found in nearby Lanarkshire. Lots of jobs were available working in shipbuilding. There was a large population around the Clyde so jobs were easily filled. Craftsmen, riveters and, later, welders were all needed to work at the shipyards. The demand for workers was so high that newly arrived immigrants, also found employment. By 1910, 80 000 people had jobs on the Clyde.

SHIPS MADE ON THE CLYDE

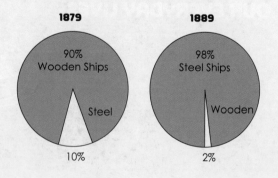

1879	1889
90% Wooden Ships / Steel 10%	98% Steel Ships / Wooden 2%

CAUSES AND IMPACT *

CTIVITIES

Use the information in the pie chart to complete the bar graph showing the increase in the number of steel and wooden ships made in Glasgow in 1889.

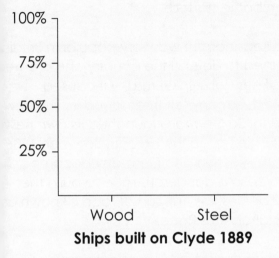

Ships built on Clyde 1889

With a partner, discuss why the Clyde specifically was so popular with shipbuilders. Try to come up with at least two reasons.

Identify the other new type of transport that was popular at the end of the nineteenth century and the start of the twentieth century. (Clue – it was also steam powered.)

Produce a poster advertising either the launch of the *Comet* or of the *Rotomanhana*. Find out about the second ship in the 'Did you know' box.

MAKE THE LINK

In **Science** we look at how the steam engine works. You could also look at the various uses of steam engines both in Science and in **Technology** classes.

In **Geography** look at how far people will travel to find work. What are the main modes of transport today as opposed to one hundred years ago? In modern society do we use technology more or less for daily transport?

In **Maths** look at how we can present statistics in line graphs, bar graphs and pie charts.

In **Technology** look at why shipbuilders changed the way they made ships. Try to find out why they stopped using rivets to build ships and started to use welding.

DID YOU KNOW?

93

The first steel ship powered by a steam engine was launched on the Clyde. The *Rotomanhana* was launched in 1879. It carried passengers and cargo between New Zealand and Melbourne, Australia. At that time she was the fastest ship in Australasia. In 1928 she was scuttled. Today many divers still visit her wreck just off the Melbourne coast.

OUR EVERYDAY LIVES

Scotland's best known comedian started his working life as a shipbuilder. Like many young men in the west of Scotland Billy Connelly started work in the shipyards. Connelly worked in the shipyards in the 1960s as a welder and boiler maker. Today Connelly is a singer, comedian and actor. Can you think of any other people who have changed jobs during their lives? Today many people have lots of different jobs in their lifetime. How many jobs do you think you will have in your lifetime?

SHIPBUILDING AND WAR

As the twentieth century began Britain was highly successful, especially in shipbuilding. However, Germany was becoming a strong country. Germany had lots of new factories and they were bulding lots of new weapons.

In 1904 the British Royal Navy appointed a new commander. Sir John Fisher became the new First Lord of the Admiralty. Fisher said that around 150 older warships needed to be scrapped as they would be useless in a modern war against Germany. He ordered the shipyards to build powerful new battleship.

HMS Dreadnought was launched in 1906. It made all other warships obsolete because it was so good. The Dreadnought was faster than any previous ship and it had thicker steel armour plating. It also had more guns and they were placed on revolving turrets. This meant it could fire in any direction and a distance of up to seven miles. Old warships needed the commander to move the ship into position before being able to fire at enemy ships. This was a difficult task, especially when the ships were powered by the wind using sails. To manoeuvre a ship in the heat of battle took a great deal of skill.

The Dreadnought had big engines. They were powered by diesel rather than steam

and this made the ship go much faster. The design of the ship was also very different to previous ships. Sailors and officers slept far closer to their action stations and this meant that there was less delay in getting ready when battle started.

The Dreadnought was very popular in Britain It helped to defend the country and created lots of new jobs. In Germany it caused panic. Germany felt threatened by this new warship. So Germany launched its own new battleship called the *Nassau*. Between 1906 and 1914 Britain and Germany became involved in a dangerous race to build the most battleships. This sort of race is known as the Naval Arms Race.

The race ended in 1914. Britain won as it launched twenty-two Dreadnoughts and Germany launched only fifteen Nassau battleships. Once the First World War started in 1914 the demand for new ships continued Many ships were sunk in battles or destroyed by German U-boats (submarines). They needed to be replaced quickly and so shipyards were kept busy during the war years from 1914 to 1918.

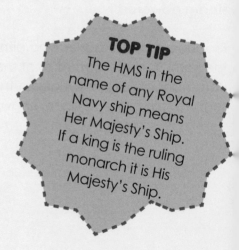

TOP TIP

The HMS in the name of any Royal Navy ship means Her Majesty's Ship. If a king is the ruling monarch it is His Majesty's Ship.

94

CTIVITIES

Make a list of all the advantages of the Dreadnought battleship.

Use the information on this page to make a bar graph which shows the number of modern battleships Britain and Germany had built by 1914.

Explain why shipbuilders were still busy even after the Naval Arms Race had come to an end in 1914.

Produce a PowerPoint presentation for the Royal Navy Admiralty. Your presentation should aim to convince them that the Royal Navy in 1906 needs to change all its ships to Dreadnoughts.

How would you convince the Admiralty to build more of these new ships?

MAKE THE LINK

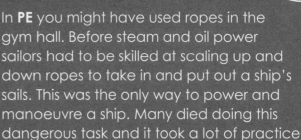

In **PE** you might have used ropes in the gym hall. Before steam and oil power sailors had to be skilled at scaling up and down ropes to take in and put out a ship's sails. This was the only way to power and manoeuvre a ship. Many died doing this dangerous task and it took a lot of practice to become skilled at the task.

In **Personal and Social Education** and in **Modern Studies** you look at what causes conflict between individual people and countries. Carrying weapons like knives, for example, can lead to a conflict because by carrying them there is a risk that they will be used. The same is true in conflicts between countries. By having a large navy, countries were running the risk of a major war. The First World War saw over one million British casualties. How would you avoid conflicts from happening in the future?

95

DID YOU KNOW?

It was a Scotsman who founded the American Navy. John Paul Jones was born in Kirkcudbrightshire in 1747. Jones served on ships from an early age. He served on ships that were involved in the Atlantic Slave Trade. During the American Revolution he fought against Britain to help gain American independence. In Britain he was seen as a pirate. On the other hand, Americans saw him as a hero.

OUR EVERYDAY LIVES

As well as the Royal Navy, Britain also has a Merchant Navy. It is the job of the Merchant Navy to make sure the Royal Navy is always supplied and British ships are protected wherever they are in the world.

THE BOOM ENDS

In 1913 some said the Clyde could not manage to build any more ships. Shipbuilding increased again during the **First World War** (1914–18). Almost half the ships ordered by the Royal Navy during the war were built on the Clyde.

There was a shortage of materials for building ships during the war. More worryingly, there was a shortage of men to work on the yards. Many men had volunteered to go and fight in the war. This caused a number of problems.

Most of the men who worked on the shipyards were members of **trade unions**. When the workers were not happy with their conditions in the shipyards they would speak to and negotiate with managers. If the managers did not listen the trade unions would call a strike. During strikes no one did any work and no ships were built. Strikes gave British shipyards a bad reputation. Customers did not get their orders on time and became fustrated. They began to take their orders elsewhere.

Another problem hit British shipyards. After the war America and Germany started to make and use new machines for building ships. British shipyards were often family run and could not afford to buy new equipment. This meant British shipyards were slower at making ships and so lost even more orders.

To help shipbuilding the German and Japanese governments gave their shipyards lots of extra money. This is called a subsidy.

Sometimes your parents or carers may subsidise something for you. The British government did not give shipyards any subsidies.

The last and maybe the most important problem for shipyards was a new invention. Aircraft started to become more popular as the century went on. Aircraft would change the way people travelled and transported goods. Soon there were fewer ship orders as people used aircraft more regularly.

Things got even worse in 1929 when all the big banks in Wall Street, New York collapsed. In the 1930s there was not a lot of money in the world and lots of people lost their jobs. This was called the Depression. It was a bad time in many factories across the world, especially shipbuilding.

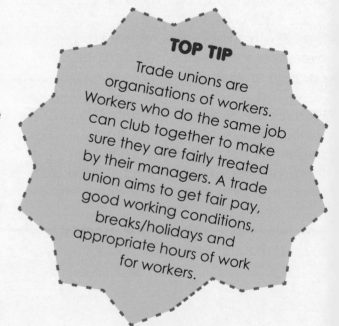

TOP TIP

Trade unions are organisations of workers. Workers who do the same job can club together to make sure they are fairly treated by their managers. A trade union aims to get fair pay, good working conditions, breaks/holidays and appropriate hours of work for workers.

CAUSES AND IMPACT *

ACTIVITIES

With a partner, discuss the feelings that shipbuilders would have at the end of the First World War. Why would they be happy? Why might they be concerned?

Make a list of the aims of a trade union.

Make a list of reasons why shipbuilding began to decline in Britain.

Make a list of reasons for the decline of British shipbuilding.

In your group discuss the reason for shipbuilding collapsing in Britain.

CAUSES AND IMPACT OF ECONOMIC CHANGE

MAKE THE LINK

In **Modern Studies** we find out more about trade unions and how they work.

In **Craft, Design and Technology** think about the materials we use to make things. If we ran out of those materials what could be used instead? Clyde shipbuilders had a shortage of materials during the war. In the modern world some materials are about to run out.

The Wall Street Crash in America had huge consequences for the whole world. In **Modern Studies,** can you think of an example of an other event in a foreign country which effected Scottish people?

DID YOU KNOW?

In 1931 a huge ship lay unfinished in the Clyde. It was to be the biggest ship in the world but the owners, Cunard, had run out of money. They could not afford to pay any workers to finish the ship. In 1934 a loan from the government meant that the ship could be finished. In 1935 the *Queen Mary* was finally launched.

OUR EVERYDAY LIVES

The term Red Clydeside refers to the fact that workers on the Clyde were often on strike during and after the First World War. Many strikers waved red flags. This represented socialism. Socialists want the government to take over factories and industries. They want workers and managers to be equal and everyone to cooperate. They do not believe people should compete with each other to make more money. In 1919 the government did not agree with this and put soldiers and tanks on the streets of Glasgow to stop the strikers.

THE STRANGE CASE OF HMS ROYAL OAK

A world war broke out again in 1939 when Adolf Hitler's Germany invaded Poland. This led to the Second World War (1939–1945). Just like in the First World War many battleships were needed. Many replacements were needed for those ships being sunk. One strange event was the sinking of *HMS Royal Oak*. On the night of 14 October 1939 over 800 men died when it sank.

The *Royal Oak* was moored in Scapa Flow in Orkney. This was a well defended base for the Royal Navy. It was apparently sunk by the German U–boat U47 commanded by Gunther Prien. Prien returned to Germany a hero. He wrote a book of his account of the events. However, not everyone agrees that Prien sunk the *Royal Oak*. Some think that it may have been a **conspiracy**. Maybe it was sunk by someone or something else. Having a massive battleship destroyed in its base so early in the war was a massive blow to British morale.

Look at the evidence below and complete the table in activity 1. History is very much like a jigsaw. Like detectives, we have to piece together lots of pieces of information to find out what happened in the past.

Scapa Flow was very well defended. Some thought it impossible to get a U-boat in.

German torpedoes from U-boat were found in the wreck by divers.

Car lights were spotted on the shore by the U-boat crew before the attack. Surely this would scare off the U-boat.

Radio signals between Navy commanders at Scapa Flow and Headquarters said it was definitely not attacked by aircraft.

Prien said the currents were strong when he escaped but all other reports say the water was calm. He could have lied about the attack.

Prien may have exaggerated his story to make him look more daring and brave.

98

CAUSES AND IMPACT *

ACTIVITIES

1 Complete the following table using the evidence from the Royal Oak.

A U-boat sunk the *Royal Oak*	Something else sunk the *Royal Oak*

2 **Decide** whether you think the *Royal Oak* was sunk by Prien or by something else. Once you have made your decision explain to others in your group how you have come to this decision.

3 Discuss with a partner what this case-study has taught you about evidence.

4 Discuss in a group what this case-study has taught you about history.

5 Explain why Gunther Prien might exaggerate his story.

6 Think what other things could have sunk the *Royal Oak* – make a list of the ideas you come up with. The difficult part is getting evidence for your ideas! But that is what being a historian is all about.

TOP TIP
A conspiracy is when something happens secretly so as to trick people into believing that something else or nothing happened

CAUSES AND IMPACT OF ECONOMIC CHANGE

MAKE THE LINK

In **English** we think about how we write or say things in a particular way to persuade people. How can you tell when someone is being biased or one sided?

In **Modern Studies** we take part in decision making exercises. We need to use this information to make an overall decision.

In **Personal and Social Education** we look at the working rights of children. We think about what jobs we can do while we are still at school and what the law says about children working. When *HMS Royal Oak* sank it had many children on board. Sailor boys were not uncommon in the Royal Navy. Try to find out what other jobs children did in the early twentieth century that would not be allowed today.

DID YOU KNOW?

99

Britain has a long, proud naval history. The song 'Rule Britannia' is about how Britain once dominated the seas because of the Royal Navy's power. Many famous naval commanders have come from Britain, Admiral Nelson being the most famous. Nelson fought during the Napoleonic Wars. Admiral Lord Duncan was a famous Scottish sea commander at the same time.

OUR EVERYDAY LIVES

Archaeologists dig under the ground to find clues about what happened in the past. There are also marine archaeologists who find clues under the sea. Today divers are not allowed on the *Royal Oak* as it is an official war grave. Scapa Flow also has a number of German warships under the sea. At the end of the First World War Germany had to surrender its navy. It scuttled its fleet in Scapa Flow. Children from Stromness witnessed the event on 21 June 1919.

SHIPBUILDING'S FINAL DECLINE

After the Second Word War ship building declined. The two countries that lost the war, Germany and Japan, were somehow making profits. In these countries the shipyards were modern. They had new ideas and new machines. This meant they were able to make more ships and quicker. Scotland had once led the world in shipbuilding. It now appeared that it was being beaten at its own game! Two major Clyde shipyards closed in the 1960s: Denny's in 1963 and Fairfields in1965. Shipbuilding had now collapsed.

Many attempts were made to save Scottish shipbuilding. The Conservative government put lots of money into the yards in the 1960s but still yards closed. The Labour government tried to save shipbuilding by taking over yards. When a government takes over a factory or an industry this is called **nationalisation.** Even this did not work. All the shipyards on the Clyde were merged into one company called Upper Clyde Shipbuilders. This was to try to cut costs and the number of workers needed. Even this did not save shipbuilding in Scotland.

Scandinavian shipyards also introduced new technology and assembly lines which sped up production. On the other hand, British yards were slow to change. Trade unions went on strike when new technology was introduced or when jobs were lost. Strikes meant that what orders Britain had for new ships were delayed. British shipyards lost many customers. Soon British companies had a bad reputation for not meeting deadlines and for lots of strikes.

Many communities along the Clyde were hit hard by the yard closures and job losses. These areas suffered badly from unemployment and depression. Men who had served long apprenticeships in the shipyards now found themselves unemployed. They had to retrain in order to gain the new skills required for other jobs. By 1985 Britain produced only 2% of the world's ships. Compare this figure to the figures earlier in the chapter.

CHALLENGE
Scotland has always been at the centre of innovation and enterprise. It has been a leading contributor to the world around us. It is up to you to take on the challenge and be the next contributors – are you up for it?

100

CAUSES AND IMPACT *

ACTIVITIES

1 Imagine you are a shipyard owner. How could you attract more orders to your shipyard? As a group come up with three ideas and try to convince your class teacher that your shipyard would be successful after the Second World War.

2 Explain what nationalisation means. Explain why the government took this step.

3 Look at the percentage at the bottom of the page opposite. Compare this to the percentage of world ships Britain made in 1900. What is the difference between 1900 and 1985.

4 Write a diary entry for a shipyard worker at Denny's in 1963. How would you feel? What sort of emotions and thoughts would be going through your mind? Your diary entry should be at least five lines long and contain at least four words which show your feelings.

MAKE THE LINK

In **Geography** we look at what other countries produce and what sort of industries they have.

In **Modern Studies** we also look at what different countries make and how the way they work is similar or different to our own country.

In **Craft, Design and Technology** we look at machines and tools from our country and other countries.

In **Enterprise** you gain the skills and a 'can do' attitude to make Scotland great.

DID YOU KNOW?

Over 70% of the world's surface is covered by seas and oceans. The sea remains very important today. See the information in the our everyday lives box.

101

OUR EVERYDAY LIVES

Today 90% of all global trade travels by sea. Coupled with the fact above, perhaps one day Scotland will return to be King of the Seas. Only you, the next generation, can make that happen! One last tip ... be active and learn the lessons from history!

BIOGRAPHIES

AGRICOLA, JULIUS B37, D93

Agricola was the Roman army general who was made governor of Britain. During that time he made several attempts to conquer North Britain or, as the Romans called it, Caledonia. Little is known about Agricola except from the biography written by his son-in-law Cornelius Tacitus. He commanded the Roman armies during the Battle of Mons Graupius.

ALEXANDER III B1241, D1286

Alexander III ruled Scotland during a time of peace with England. Relations between the two countries were good with rich trade links being set up. The period under Alexander III's rule is often called 'the Golden Age'. However, he led a sad life, with his two sons, his daughter and first wife dying. Alexander's reign was brought to a sudden end in 1286 when he fell off his horse and died at Kinghorn, near Fife.

BALLIOL, JOHN B1249, D1313

He became the king after the death of Alexander III. Balliol was chosen by King Edward I of England over Robert Bruce. Balliol's claim to the throne was that he was a descendant of David I. Balliol refused to send Scottish soldiers to King Edward's war in France. After he saw the English attack Berwick, steal the Stone of Destiny, steal the Crown Jewels and remove his royal robes. Balliol left Scotland for France never to return to his throne.

BRUCE, ROBERT THE B1274, D1329

His grandfather had a strong claim to the Scottish throne after Alexander III died. During the early part of the Scottish Wars of Independence Bruce fought on the English side and may even have fought against Wallace at Falkirk. He is believed to have been involved in the murder of John Comyn in 1306. After skilfully taking back the castles he won an important victory over the English at Bannockburn in 1314. In 1328 Edward III of England formally recognised him as King of Scotland. Bruce died in 1329. His body is buried at Dunfermline Abbey and his heart is buried at Melrose Abbey.

EDWARD I OF ENGLAND B1239 D1307

He is often called the Hammer of the Scots. He tried to establish a united Britain by conquering England's neighbours. He helped choose Scotland's next king after Alexander III died and then went to war against Scotland and Wales.

ELIZABETH I B1533, D1603

Elizabeth had a traumatic early life as her mother, Anne Boleyn, was executed when Elizabeth was only three. Anne Boleyn was Henry VIII's second wife. Elizabeth is sometimes called the Virgin Queen as she had no children to inherit her throne. The next in line to crown her was Mary Queen of Scots. Elizabeth did not want Mary to inherit the throne as Mary was a Catholic. Many Catholics did not think Elizabeth should have inherited the English throne as Henry had divorced his wife (he had six wives in total!).

HADRIAN B76, D138

Hadrian was the Roman Emperor who had a huge defensive wall built in his name to stop Celtic attacks on Roman Britain. It was the largest defence in the Roman Empire and ran for 117 kilometers.

KNOX, JOHN B C1512 D1572

John Knox studied at St Andrews University and initially worked for the Catholic Church. He began to work with and become close to George Wishart. Wishart was part of the Reformation movement that was bringing Protestantism to Scotland. Knox was in St Andrews at the time of the murder of a Catholic Cardinal, Cardinal Beaton. For this he was punished by being sent to work on an oar aboard a French galley ship. He later returned to Scotland. He preached the Protestant faith and was greatly opposed to Mary Queen of Scots.

SELLAR, PATRICK B1780, D1851

Sellar is often seen as the man who carried out the Highland Clearances, but he was in fact only responsible for Clearances in the area owned by the 1st Duke of Sutherland. Sellar was in charge of evictions when a house went on fire in Strathnaver. Inverness High Court acquitted him.

TACITUS B56 D117

Tacitus was the son-in-law of Roman General Agricola. He was a Roman senator (politician) and a historian. He wrote a famous biography about his father-in-law's triumphs, which gives us much information about Roman attacks on Scotland and also the Celtic tribes who defeated them.

MACALPIN, KENNETH B C800, D858

MacAlpin is often credited with being the first king of Scotland. However, he only united the Picts of northern Scotland and the Gaels who lived in the Dalriada area in the west. Other parts of Scotland remained separate. Despite this he was the first king to bring together major areas and peoples of a then divided land. He saw off Viking raids in 843. Recently, documents have been found which show that Kenneth's youngest son, Aed, may have been the first king of a united Scotland.

MARGARET MAID OF NORWAY B1283, D1290

Margaret was the daughter of Erik II of Norway and the granddaugher of Alexander III of Scotland. When Alexander died in 1286 Margaret fell heir to the throne of Scotland. There was much concern given that she was a female ruler, only an infant and lived in Norway. Until she was old enough to rule, Scotland was to be ruled by a group of nobles called the Guardians of Scotland. On her journey from Norway to Scotland in 1290 she fell ill and the ships had to stop at Orkney. There she died, having never set foot on the Scottish mainland.

103

MARY QUEEN OF SCOTS B1542, D1587

Mary inherited the Throne from her father, James V, during very difficult times for Scotland. She had to face challenges to her authority from nobles and religious opponents. She continued to worship the Catholic faith at a time when many Scots converted to Protestantism. She married three times. Her first husband, Francis the Dauphin, died. Her second husband, Lord Darnley, was murdered and her third husband, Bothwell, ended up imprisoned in a Danish jail. Mary tried to escape from her enemies by moving towards her cousin in England. Elizabeth signed her death warrent and had her head chapped off.

NAPIER, DAVID B1790, D1869

Napier built engines and boilers for ships, most famously for the *Comet*. His family were engineers. He was to become very successful in steamship building. His company ran steamer services in the west of Scotland and to Belfast. They used iron ships and steam power.

NAPIER, ROBERT B1791, D1876

Robet Napier was David Napier's cousin. He is sometimes referred to as 'the father of shipbuilding'. His company was one of the first to produce all iron ships. His company include *HMS Jackal* in 1841. This was the first iron warships. He also built passenger ships for companies like Cunard. In 1849 he built the world's first train ferry, the *Leviathan*. He became a very powerful businessman in Scotland.

PATERSON, WILLIAM B1658, D1719

Paterson traded in the West Indies. He suggested the setting up of the Bank of England. He was one of the Bank's first directors. Paterson was very keen for Scotland to have similar success. He backed the Company of Scotland and the Darien Scheme. The Scheme ended in disaster for the Company, for Scotland and for Paterson. The expeditions to Darien were a failure and Scotland lost a number of lives and a lot of money. Paterson lost his second wife and son at the same time. He later supported the Act of Union and was compensated for the money he lost in the Darien disaster.

STEWART, CHARLES EDWARD (THE YOUNG PRETENDER) B1720, D1788

He was the son of the Old Pretender and the grandson of James VII and II. Nicknamed Bonnie Prince Charlie, he led the Jacobite Rebellion in 1745 which ended in defeat at Culloden in 1746. He had to hide from government soldiers in the Highlands and eventually escaped to France.

STEWART, JAMES FRANCIS (THE OLD PRETENDER) B1688 D1766

He was the only son of James VII and I and was exiled to France with his family in 1688. After the death of Queen Anne, James felt he should have been made King. However the Act of Succession ensured that a protestant would inherit the throne from Anne would be Protestant. This meant that George of Hanover became the next king despite being 52nd in line to the throne. Believing he should be king, James gained the nickname 'The Old Pretender'. Supporters of his cause were called Jacobites. They launched failed attempts to get the 'Old Pretender' onto the throne. He spent most of his later life in exile in Catholic Rome.

WATT, JAMES B1736, D1819

Watt was an inventor who developed a new and more efficient steam engine. His inventions were used in factories, coal mines and in transport all over the world.

WALLACE, WILLIAM BORN C1270, D1305

Wallace is best known for defeating the English at Stirling Bridge and becoming the Guardian of Scotland. Later, Wallace was defeated at Falkirk and then betrayed by a fellow Scot. He was put on trial in London and found guilty of crimes of treason against Edward I. He was hanged, drawn and quartered and he became a martyr figure in Scotland.

WATT, JAMES

ACTIVITIES

FAMOUS SCOTS TIMELINE

Use the biography section to put the key people we have studied in this book into chronological order. The first and the last ones have been done for you.

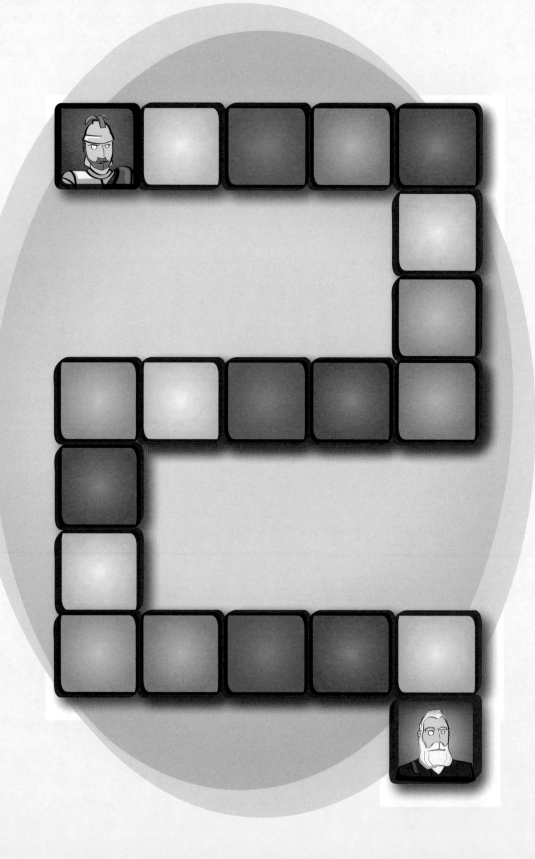

ACTIVITIES

HIGHS AND LOWS

Use this graph to record Scotland's highs and lows

First choose ten key dates in Scottish history. Put these along the x axis. They must be in chronological order.

Then show if the events were happy ones or sad ones for Scotland by marking them on the graph as either happy (near the top) or sad (near the bottom).

AND NOW TRY

You could make different graphs for different groups of people. For example, one for kings, one for farmers, one for shipbuilders. Some people will feel very differently about the same event. Think about how different Scottish people felt about the return of Mary Queen of Scots.

ACTIVITIES

MAPPING SCOTLAND'S HISTORY

You should use this map to identify where the key moments in Scottish history took place. Go through the Course Notes and make a list of events. Then, mark these on your map. Some have already been done for you.

You may want to ask your teacher to make this map A3 size so that you have more space to put on all the events you have found.

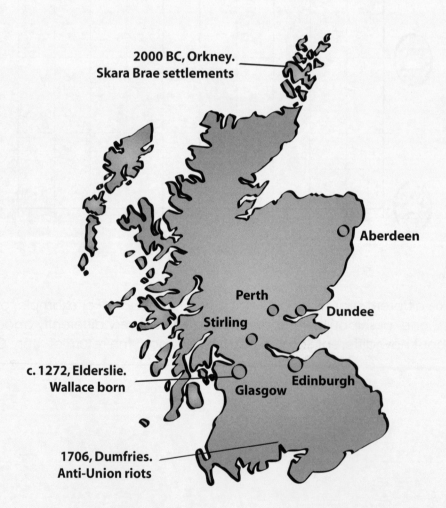

2000 BC, Orkney.
Skara Brae settlements

Aberdeen

Perth

Dundee

Stirling

c. 1272, Elderslie.
Wallace born

Glasgow

Edinburgh

1706, Dumfries.
Anti-Union riots

ACTIVITIES

SCOTLAND AND THE WORLD

Use this map to mark on all the connections Scotland has in the world. You can mark on places Scots went to, connections Scotland has had with other countries or even places where new Scots have come from. How many connections can you make?

You might want to ask your teacher to make this map A3 size so that you have more space to mark on all the connections.

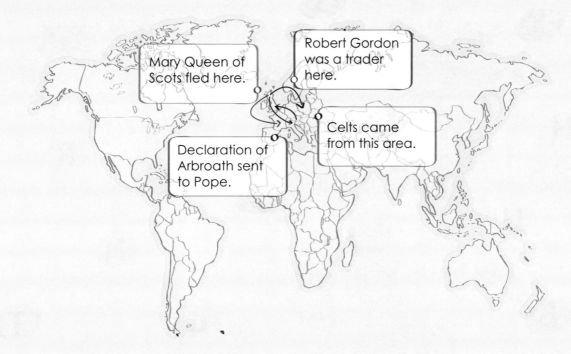

109

ACTIVITIES

THE BIG A–Z CHALLENGER

Earlier in this book you used the A–Z to help you remember people, places and events in the Highland Clearances chapter. Now use this A–Z to show your knowledge on all the topics we have studied in this book. Which letter can you find the most words for? (For example: A – Act of Union, Y – Young Pretender.)

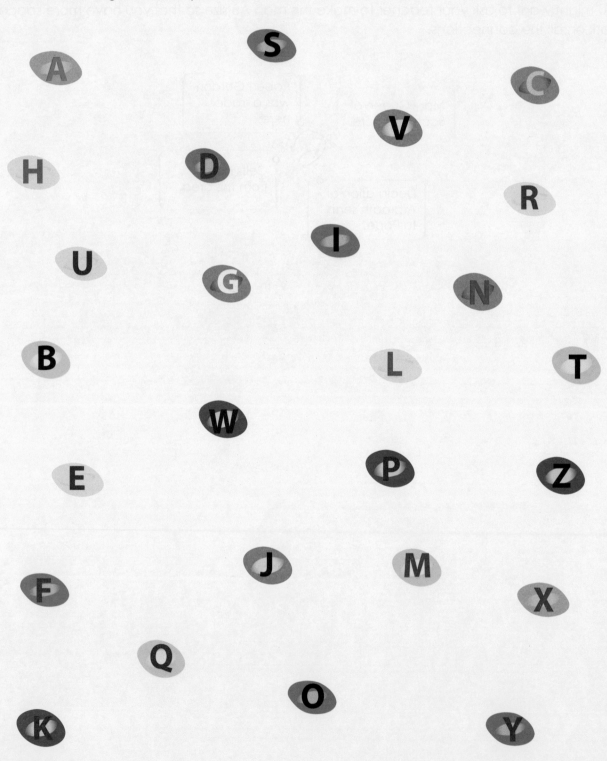

ACTIVITIES

ENTERPRISING MINDS

Work with a partner for this exercise. On this page are some objects which have appeared in this book. Your job is to come up with as many uses as you can for each item. For example, consider the straw cart used at Linlithgow by Robert the Bruce. It can be used as a straw cart and a barricade. However, we could also use it as a chariot, a mobile shop, a children's ride. It is a matter of letting your imagination run wild! Have a try for yourself.

Once you have come up with as many uses for each item as you can, link up with another pair and share your ideas. Then link up with another two pairs to see what they have come up with. What is the best idea your class can come up with for each one?